Get Rid of your Accent
Part One and Two

GENERAL AMERICAN
SPEECH TRAINING MANUAL

By Linda James and Olga Smith

ISBN: 9780955330087

Published by Olga Smith, Business & Technical Communication Services Global
8 Fairholme Road, London, W14 9JX, United Kingdom

Information on this title and accent reduction courses: www.batcsglobal.com

First Edition

Table of Contents

Introduction

What is an accent?

An accent identifies which part of the country or world you come from. There are different types of accents: Southern, German, French, Spanish, educated, strong, slight and many others.

Why do we speak with different accents?

From our childhood we learn to speak by imitating our relatives, teachers and friends. The way we speak and our pronunciation are influenced by the environment in which we live.

Sounds are created by our speech organs, namely lips, tongue and jaw. Positions of our speech organs are different for different sounds. For example, we drop the tongue in order to pronounce the English [æ] sound as in "cat". In order to pronounce [w] as in "way" we put our lips in a tight whistle, and then pull them back sharply.

Many people begin to learn English when they are adults. They may not automatically position their speech organs as native English speakers will. Moreover, they often don't know how to correctly position their speech organs in order to produce clear English sounds because not all English sounds exist in other languages.

For example, there is no [w] in Russian, and many Russians pronounce [v] instead of [w]. Another example is that in Russian they don't have long vowels, and therefore there is a natural tendency for Russians to shorten long English vowels and diphthongs. Instead of "two sheets of paper" they most likely will pronounce "two shits of paper". Instead of saying "the room is dark", they are likely to pronounce "the room is duck".

Speaking, writing and listening are taught in most colleges, but phonetics and pronunciation classes are not always part of the curriculum, and even when they are, they tend to be very basic and focus more on conversation than phonetics.

1

Is it important to have good pronunciation?

Just consider the following points:

Bad pronunciation:
- May be confusing and hard to understand for those who listen to you
- Gives the impression that you are uneducated
- Doesn't allow you to become a good public speaker.

Good pronunciation and a neutral accent:
- Allows you to become a pleasant communicator
- Is a good basis for public speaking
- Will enable you to enjoy speaking more
- Gives you confidence, and your confidence in turn opens up for you all sorts of opportunities.

Is it possible to reduce or eliminate an accent?

The earlier we start to pronounce English properly, the less accent we have. It's more difficult to reduce or completely eliminate an accent when you are older. However, it is not impossible. It all depends on your hard work, perseverance, high quality professional training, and – last, but not least – on using the appropriate book with a sound track.

What accent do we teach? Does General American English exist?

Why not learn to speak with a Southern or Bronx accent? Why make an effort to reduce a strong Spanish or Chinese accent? The reason is very simple: to help you make your English clear and easy to understand to the majority of English-speaking people.

This book teaches you how to a neutral pronunciation of English as spoken by educated Americans. Some refer to it as General American, GA.

We have conducted an extensive research into what GA actually is. Our finding revealed that there is more than one model for General American sounds, particularly when it comes to [ɔ] as in "saw" and [ɑ] as in "father" sounds.

GA is evolving and changing, what wasn't acceptable five years ago became a norm today. We relied on a tried and trusted Daniel Jones dictionary which is respected by all American dialect coaches and is the only source of consistency in learning an educated American Accent. The quote below proves our findings.

"We know that large differences exist in the pronunciation of vowels depending upon geographic region and other demographic variables. Although we use the term General American English, it is doubtful that such a general model truly exist." (CloperPisoni and de Jong, 2005)

Why we wrote this book

There are many books on the market that teach pronunciation. What we found is that some books are good for theory and an introduction to learning the sounds, but they did not include enough practical exercises.

In our book we made sure that students have many examples of words, sentences and verses for each particular sound. The exercises are quite intensive and will require you to work hard at your pronunciation. Students will find that our compact, concise approach makes it very accessible and easy to use. The book isn't just a study tool; we have also tried to make it amusing and interesting. Have fun, and remember that your hard work will be rewarded in full!

Three things that make our book special

- Tried and trusted method in eliminating an accent
- Fun yet very effective speech training
- Humorous vocabulary
- Compact, concise format
- Practical approach that works

Methodology used in this book

In our book, we set out a complete method of learning English sounds, many of which may not be present in a student's native language.

One of the important things about our book is that we make it absolutely clear what is happening in the mouth: where the lips go, where the tongue is placed, if the jaw is open or closed, etc. Once

3

those three positions are checked and sorted out then there is no way that you could not make that particular English sound.

The second important part of speech training is training the muscles of the tongue, lips and jaw, so that the brain memory responds to it automatically. You train them by pronouncing words and sentences with a target sound. You finish with a short verse, something interesting and amusing, but also containing a target sound.

For consonants we also give practice through articulation exercises, such as period verses and tongue-twisters, which get the tongue and the lips really moving so that we get clarity and crispness of speech. English is a very energetic and dynamic language and good articulation makes a big difference.

Exercises in the book are accompanied by a sound track on the AUDIO TRACKS. Students should listen to the AUDIO TRACKS, practice the correct sound throughout and then record themselves and listen to the recording in order to see their progress. We also encourage students to use the correct sounds in their everyday speech and support it by additional exercises at the end of each lesson.

The AUDIO TRACKS was recorded by professional actors who used drama techniques in order to make the sentences, verses and poems sound interesting and amusing. This also helps you to imagine what you are reading and that will help you to memorize sounds.

The lessons in this book are quite intensive and are aimed for those who strive to achieve outstanding results in improving their accents within a short period of time. Your results might depend on your ability to hear your own speech and the time you spend mastering the sounds.

At the end of the book we also provide students with instructions and advice on how to maintain correct pronunciation. In support of that we give a warm-up exercise for all the English sounds (see page 127).

Students will also find a table of particular difficulties with the English pronunciation which speakers of other world languages have (see page 131).

English spelling and pronunciation

In many languages letters of the alphabet are pronounced in the same way as they are spelled. However, the English language was, at different times, under French, German and Dutch influence. Because of this, the English language includes many foreign words. This is one of the reasons why there are so many exceptions to the rule in pronunciation and spelling.

The characteristic peculiarity of the English language is that the same letter of the alphabet can be pronounced differently. For example, the letter "a" in the word "father" is pronounced as a long vowel [ɑː], but in the word "man" it is a short vowel sound [æ]. In the word "among", where it's not stressed, it is a neutral vowel or schwa [ə]. Thus the letter "a" can be pronounced in at least three different ways.

Another difficulty is that the same English sounds have different spellings. For example, diphthong [ɪə] has several spellings: in the word 'fear' it is spelled as 'ear', in the word 'weird' it is spelled as 'eir'.

Although we highlight the practiced sound in bold type and offer different spelling variations for the same sound, we should point out that there can be other spelling variations that we haven't included. Therefore, when you learn a new word you should always consult a dictionary for the correct phonetic pronunciation.

Who this book is for

This book is ideal for those who already achieved an Intermediate or level of English, but even the beginners would benefit by learning how to pronounce the words and have fun with funny tongue twisters and verses.

We run courses using our books and people who come to us are professionals, diplomats, students, business people for whom good speech is important.

Method of learning

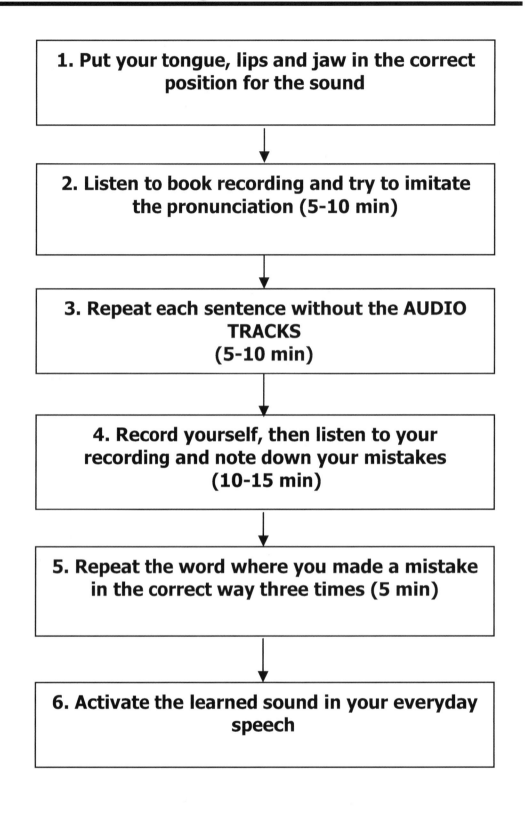

1. Put your tongue, lips and jaw in the correct position for the sound

2. Listen to book recording and try to imitate the pronunciation (5-10 min)

3. Repeat each sentence without the AUDIO TRACKS (5-10 min)

4. Record yourself, then listen to your recording and note down your mistakes (10-15 min)

5. Repeat the word where you made a mistake in the correct way three times (5 min)

6. Activate the learned sound in your everyday speech

Explanation of the method of learning

What is needed to start working with the App?
- a mirror, to compare the shape of your own mouth to the shape of the mouth that you will find in diagrams at the beginning of each lesson;
- a Smart phone, or tablet, or a PC;

See page 123 for a labelled diagram of speech organs.

How many hours you should spend on each sound:
- Practice each sound for about 20-40 minutes a day, with little breaks in between;
- Repeat on the following days for approximately the same length of time until you feel that you can use the correct sound in your everyday speech.

As shown on the previous page, the method of learning is based on a six-stage process:

The first stage is to make sure that you put your lips, tongue and jaw in the right position for the learned sound. If you fail to do so, the sound will not be precise and may be different altogether. Follow the instructions on speech organ position given at the beginning of each lesson. Pronounce the sound several times looking in the mirror to make sure you do it correctly. When you feel that your sound is correct, start pronouncing the words, sentences and verses in the lesson.

The second stage is aimed at helping you learn a sound by repeating and imitating after the tape. This exercise will help you to make the sound as correctly as possible and train your speech organs for the particular sound. The more you repeat after the tape, the better your pronunciation becomes.

The third stage gives you an opportunity to practice the sound on your own, without the help of the tape. You will be hearing yourself and mastering the sound. This stage is essential before recording yourself.

The fourth stage involves recording yourself and listening to the recording. It helps you to see whether you have progressed in mastering the pronunciation and to identify where you still make mistakes.

The fifth stage focuses on eliminating mistakes. Correctly repeating the words where you made a mistake will help you avoid repeating the same mistakes in the future.

The sixth stage has the purpose of helping you incorporate the learned sound in everyday speech. It's about trying to find the learned sound in the newspapers, on the radio, on TV and in English language videos. Pay attention to how you pronounce the learned sound in your everyday speech. This will help you to activate the correctly pronounced sounds.

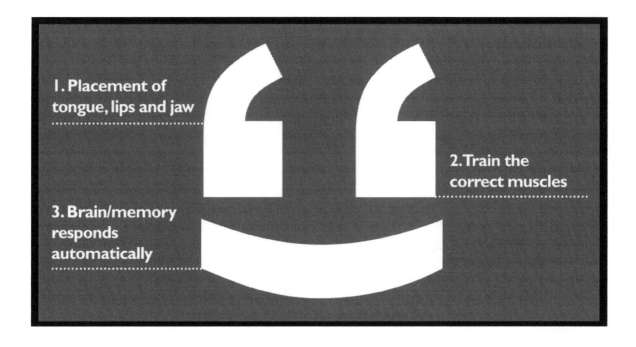

Intonation

Intonation/inflexion is a gentle rise and fall of the voice within a sentence. Experienced speech tutors have come to the conclusion that it's very challenging to teach, because each person will involuntarily assume the tune of their native language. It is very deeply ingrained in a person. Emotion and meaning will inevitably change the levels of pitch in the voice. Learners of General American are advised to listen to native English speakers on audio books, AUDIO TRACKSs, at the movies, in the theatre etc., and try to copy not only the pronunciation, but also the tune of the voice, or intonation.

Stress

The English language is composed of words with varied stresses. All words when said in isolation, and most words when in a connected passage, have at least one stressed syllable. When we combine words into sentences, the words retain their individual stress, but because of the meaning the speaker wants to convey certain complete words are stressed. For example:

1. Linda walked to the theatre with Michael. By putting a stress on "Michael", we emphasise that Linda walked to the theatre with Michael, and not John or somebody else.

2. Linda walked to the theatre with Michael. By putting a stress on "walked" we emphasise that Linda walked to the theatre, and did not, for example, ride or cycle.

3. Linda walked to the theatre with Michael. By putting a stress on "theatre", we emphasise that Linda walked to the theatre, and not to the cinema or a concert.

4. Linda walked to the theatre with Michael. By putting a stress on "Linda", we emphasise that it was Linda who walked to the theatre with Michael, and not somebody else.

The above examples demonstrate that sentence stress depends on the meaning we wish to convey and that there is no particular rule to follow. Stress comes from a combination of several factors – extra loudness of sounds, extra length of sounds and a change of pitch in the voice.

The Phonemic Alphabet

Vowels

[ɑ] as in "father"
[ɑʳ] as in "car"
[u] as in "beauty"
[ɔʳ] as in "horse"
[i] as in "feet"
[ɜʳ] as in "third"
[ə] neutral vowel (schwa) as in "the"
[əʳ]coloured schwa as in "doctor"
[ʌ] as in "duck"
[e] as in "pen"
[ɛʳ] as in "care"
[ʊ] as in "book"
[ʊʳ]ʳas in "poor"
[æ] as in "cat"

Diphthongs

[oʊ] as in "home"
[eɪ] as in "cake"
[ɔɪ] as in "boy"
[ɪə] as in "theater"
[ɪəʳ] as in "dear"
[aɪ] as in "bride"
[aʊ] as in "cow"

Semi-vowels

[j] as in "yacht"
[w] as in "want"

Consonants

[p] as in "pack"
[b] as in "big"
[t] as in "tick"
[d] as in "dog"

[k] as in "kind"
[g] as in "gloss"
[m] as in "monk"
[n] as in "nun"
[ŋ] as in "king"
[l] as in "link"
[f] as in "fun"
[v] as in "victory"
[θ] as in "think"
[ð] as in "mother"
[s] as in "son"
[z] as in "zigzag"
[ʃ] as in "shock" and voiced [ʒ] as in "vision"
[h] as in "hat"
[r] sound as in "rat"
[tʃ] as in "church"
[dʒ] as in "gin"

Lesson 1: The [ɑ] sound as in "balm"

Speech organs position:
Open jaw, relaxed lips;
flat tongue pulled back a little.
The sound is made in the back
of the mouth.

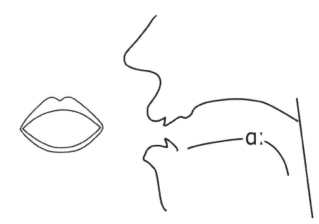

[ɑ   ɑ   ɑ]

A1
🎧 **Words**

Spelling variations for the [ɑ] sound	Highlighted bold letters pronounced as [ɑː]
o	h**o**tmail, d**o**t, c**o**m, f**o**llow, f**o**nd, kn**o**ck, m**o**b, ap**o**logy, pr**o**mise, p**o**pular, g**o**ssip, c**o**py, f**o**ssils, st**o**p, m**o**dern, n**o**t, pr**o**fit,
a	f**a**ther, c**a**lm, b**a**lm, **a**lmond, p**a**lm, ps**a**lms, renaiss**a**nce

A2
🎧 **Sentences**

1. Sl**o**ppy d**o**ctor Sc**o**tt **o**perated **o**n a little t**o**t.
2. A l**o**t of **o**dd d**o**cuments are l**o**cked in the b**o**x.
3. Can I p**o**ssibly w**a**sh my c**o**tton s**o**cks in this **o**dd p**o**nd?
4. Pr**o**blem s**o**lved – I g**o**t t**o**p d**o**llar for my b**o**nd!
5. I felt **o**dd when frisked from t**o**p to b**o**ttom by a h**o**stile c**o**p.
6. It was **o**bvious why t**o**p c**o**llege students g**o**t their j**o**bs.
7. A nice **a**lmond b**a**lm was c**a**lming for my f**a**ther's sore arm.
8. A h**o**t bl**o**nd m**o**del was sp**o**tted in the B**o**dy Sh**o**p.

A3

🎧 **Verses**

Doctor Potter had a problem,
He never got his way,
He left for Oxford but landed in Oxnard,
And there he decided to stay.

Additional exercises:

A: *Write down 4 words with the target sound that you often use when speaking English. Practice these words, thinking about your lips, tongue and jaw positions for the target sound.*

1. _____ 3. _____

2. _____ 4. _____

B: *Write down 4 words with the target sound that you often hear on TV, radio or from your friends/colleagues. Practice these words, thinking about your lips, tongue and jaw positions for the target sound.*

1. _____ 3. _____

2. _____ 4. _____

Lesson 2: The sound [ɑʳ] as in "bark"

Speech organs position:
Open jaw, relaxed lips. Start with flat tongue pulled back a little as in lesson 1, then curl the tip of the tongue up for [r] sound.

[ɑʳ   ɑʳ   ɑʳ]

A4
🎧 **Words**

Spelling variations for the [ɑʳ] sound	Highlighted bold letters pronounced as [ɑʳ]
ar	**ar**t, **ar**ms, b**ar**, m**ar**k, c**ar**t, c**ar**d, st**ar**t, **ar**t, m**ar**ble, l**ar**ge, ch**ar**ge, b**ar**k, p**ar**sley, p**ar**ty, b**ar**gain, m**ar**gin, t**ar**get, h**ar**d, **ar**gue, ch**ar**ge
ear, er	h**ear**t, s**er**geant

A5
🎧 **Sentences**

1. Let's p**ar**k our **car** not f**ar** from B**ar**bara's f**ar**m.
2. H**ar**d-h**ear**ted M**ar**garet was st**ar**tled by st**ar**s in the d**ar**k.
3. It's very h**ar**d but we must p**ar**t. I'm off to see my b**ar**ber.
4. Prior to st**ar**ting at H**ar**vard, B**ar**nie p**ar**tied h**ar**d with an **ar**my s**er**geant.
5. **Ar**thur's rem**ar**ks were truly from the h**ear**t.

A6
🎧 **Verses**

B**ar**bara's **car** is a Jagu**ar**
And B**ar**bara drives rather fast.
Castles, f**ar**ms and drafty b**ar**ns,
She goes ch**ar**ging past.

14

When I, good friends, was called to the b**ar**,
I'd an appetite fresh and h**ear**ty,
But I was, as many barristers **are**,
An impecunious p**ar**ty.
(W.S. Gilbert)

Additional exercises:

A: *Write down 4 words with the target sound that you often use when speaking English. Practice these words, thinking about your lips, tongue and jaw positions for the target sound.*

1. _____ 3. _____

2. _____ 4. _____

B: *Write down 4 words with the target sound that you often hear on TV, radio or from your friends/colleagues. Practice these words, thinking about your lips, tongue and jaw positions for the target sound.*

1. _____ 3. _____

2. _____ 4. _____

Lesson 3: The [u] sound as in "boot"

Speech organs position:
Jaw is almost closed,
lips pushed forward tightly
into a whistle shape;
the back of the tongue
rises up towards the soft
palate at the back of the mouth.

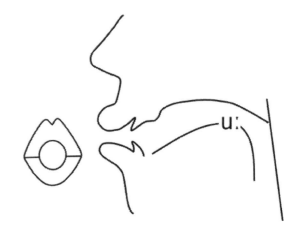

[u   u   u]

A7
🎧 **Words**

Spelling variations for the [u] sound	Highlighted bold letters pronounced as [u]
oo	bl**oo**m, f**oo**d, sm**oo**th, l**oo**p, sch**oo**l, d**oo**m
o	l**o**se, m**o**ve, d**o**, wh**o**, impr**o**vement, rem**o**ve
ue, oe	bl**ue**, gl**ue**, sh**oe**s
ui	fr**ui**t, j**ui**ce, cr**ui**se
Spelling variations for the [ju] sound	Highlighted bold letters pronounced as [ju]
u	m**u**sic, m**u**se
ew	n**ew**, f**ew**, m**ew**s

A8
🎧 **Sentences**

1. R**u**th sat on a st**oo**l in the c**oo**l of a J**u**ne evening and admired the b**eau**ty of the m**oo**n.
2. These n**ew** bl**ue** sh**oe**s look b**eau**tiful with a navy bl**ue** coat.
3. On our cr**ui**se to Berm**u**da we played p**oo**l with our sch**oo**ner cr**ew**.

4. A f**ew** b**eau**tiful bl**ue**bells gr**ew** in the sch**oo**l garden in J**u**ly.
5. "A f**oo**l and his money are s**oo**n parted." *(Proverb)*

A9

🎧 Verses

We sail the ocean bl**ue**,
And our saucy ship's a b**eau**ty;
We're sober men and tr**ue**,
And attentive to our b**eau**ty.

When Romeo met Juliet by the light of the m**oo**n,
He swore he'd pr**o**ve he'd always be tr**ue**,
Alas their love was over too s**oo**n,
But their story lives on, as tr**ue** love will d**o**.

Additional exercises:

A: *Write down 4 words with the target sound that you often use when speaking English. Practice these words, thinking about your lips, tongue and jaw positions for the target sound.*

1. _____ 3. _____

2. _____ 4. _____

B: *Write down 4 words with the target sound that you often hear on TV, radio or from your friends/colleagues. Practice these words, thinking about your lips, tongue and jaw positions for the target sound.*

1. _____ 3. _____

2. _____ 4. _____

Lesson 4: The sound [ɔ] as in "daughter"

Speech organs position:
The lips slightly rounded in oval shape, nearly flat tongue, with back of tongue slightly rising. Open jaw.

[ɔ   ɔ   ɔ]

A10
🎧 Words

Listen and repeat. Look at the mouth diagram to help you position your lips, tongue and jaw for the target sound.

Spelling variations for the [ɑ] sound	Highlighted bold letters pronounced as [ɑ:]
aw, au, ow, aw	l**aw**, l**aw**n, s**aw**, c**au**se, f**au**lt, **Au**gust, p**aw**n, **au**thor, **au**dition, v**au**lt
ough, augh	f**ough**t, th**ough**tful, c**augh**t, t**augh**t,
a before **l**	b**all**, w**all**, f**all**, **al**ways, c**all**, **al**ready, sm**all**
o	al**o**ng, s**o**ng, c**o**st, acr**o**ss, c**o**ffee, s**o**rry

A11
🎧 Comparison: [ɑ] as in "balm" and [ɔ] as in "daughter"

[ɑ]   [ɔ]

[ɑ]	[ɔ]	[ɑ]	[ɔ]
bond	**bough**t	p**o**pular	f**all**
lock	lost	project	soft
rock	wr**o**ng	contract	c**au**tious
clock	c**all**	economy	**al**ways
knock	n**augh**ty	copy	c**augh**t
promise	appl**au**d	modern	t**al**k
politics	**au**thor	profit	loss
policy	c**au**se	comment	**al**ready

18

A12
🎧 **Sentences**

1. Cl**au**de was f**a**lling asleep **aw**kwardly in a spr**aw**l.
2. The written l**aw**s **ough**t to prevent th**ough**tless t**a**lks.
3. P**au**l's d**au**ghter P**au**line was an **aw**ful d**au**ghter-in-l**aw**.
4. P**au**l c**a**lled out when he th**ou**ght he s**aw** his n**au**ghty d**au**ghter f**a**ll in the w**a**ter.
5. We had c**o**ffee with some t**o**ffee and a s**au**sage roll.
6. My b**o**ss had an **aw**ful c**ou**gh during our exh**au**sting l**o**ng c**a**ll.
7. When our h**augh**ty b**o**ss is g**o**ne we t**a**lk about him **a**ll day l**o**ng.

A13
🎧 **Verse**

Listen and copy the intonation and voice modulation on the AUDIO TRACKS.

Cl**au**de p**au**sed in a l**o**ng h**a**ll and leaned against a t**a**ll w**a**ll.
He did not want his shopping bags to f**a**ll.
Then he t**a**lked to his d**augh**ter about **a**ll he b**ough**t,
It was **aw**esome to know what his d**au**ghter th**ough**t!

Bibby Bobby b**ough**t a bat; Bibby Bobby b**ough**t a b**a**ll,
With that bat he banged the b**a**ll, banged it bump against the w**a**ll,
But so boldly Bobby banged, soon he burst the rubber b**a**ll.
Boo sobbed Bobby, goodbye b**a**ll. Bad luck, Bobby, bad luck b**a**ll.
Now to drown his many troubles, Bibby Bobby's blowing bubbles!

Lesson 5: The sound [ɔʳ] as in "horse"

Speech organs position:
The lips are coming forward a little, but not tight; the jaw is reasonably relaxed and quite open. The back of the tongue is slightly lifted. Then the tip of the tongue curls up for the [r] sound.

[ɔʳ   ɔʳ   ɔʳ]

A14
🎧 **Words**

Spelling variations for the [ɔʳ] sound	Highlighted bold letters pronounced as [ɔʳ]
or, our	st**or**m, c**our**se, b**or**ed, **sor**e, c**our**t, **or**ange, c**or**porate, **for**, **or**der, rep**or**t, imp**or**tant, c**or**ner, c**our**se, m**or**e, aff**or**d, w**or**ship
ar	w**ar**, w**ar**drobe, w**arr**ant, w**ar**m, w**ar**ship

A15
🎧 **Sentences**

Listen and repeat. Read each sentence aloud slowly at first, then as if you were telling it to someone in a natural way.

1. To make a long story sh**or**t, this is m**or**e than I can aff**or**d.
2. The owner of the c**or**ner st**or**e was an extra**or**dinary b**or**e.
3. **Four** hundred and f**or**ty-f**our** st**or**ks flew home in the st**or**m.
4. Ge**or**ge's h**or**se ate **four** **or**ganic c**oar**se straws.
5. The h**or**ns in an **or**chestra number **four**; never less, and never m**or**e.
6. "Don't shut the stable d**oor** after the h**or**se has bolted." *(Proverb)*

A16
🎧 **Verses**

Listen and copy the intonation and voice modulation on the AUDIO TRACKS.

Gordon St**or**ner from the day he was b**or**n,
Always wanted to play the h**or**n,
He practised and practised from early m**or**n,
But still never managed to master that h**or**n!

Additional exercises:

A: *Write down 4 words with the target sound that you often use when speaking English. Practice these words, thinking about your lips, tongue and jaw positions for the target sound.*

1. _____ 3. _____

2. _____ 4. _____

B: *Write down 4 words with the target sound that you often hear on TV, radio or from your friends/colleagues. Practice these words, thinking about your lips, tongue and jaw positions for the target sound.*

1. _____ 3. _____

2. _____ 4. _____

Lesson 6: The [i] sound as in "feet"

Speech organs position:
Jaw is almost closed,
lips are spread; the front of
the tongue is high and forward
in the mouth.

[i   i   i]

A17
🎧 Words

Spelling variations for the [iː] sound	Highlighted bold letters pronounced as [iː]
ee	keel, feeble, seek, heed, see, peep, feel
e	he, evening, eve, demonize, Peter, these
ea	meat, tea, leave, jeans, please, team, neat
ie	grief, field, relief, believe
ei	receipt, deceit, seize

A18
🎧 Sentences

1. One **e**v**e**ning, lying by the str**ea**m on the gr**ee**n grass, I dr**ea**med of **ea**ting Gr**ee**k ch**ee**se.
2. J**ea**n, have you b**ee**n in a wh**ea**t f**ie**ld this w**ee**k?
3. "All l**e**gal furies s**ei**ze you! No proposal s**ee**ms to pl**ea**se you."
4. I bel**ie**ve my f**ee**t are really quite cl**ea**n, **E**v**ie**.
5. "A new broom sw**ee**ps cl**ea**n." *(Proverb)*

A19
🎧 **Verses**

S**ee** – s**ee** – they drink
All thought unh**ee**ding,
The t**ea**-cups clink,
They are exc**ee**ding!

It s**ee**ms to me you're very k**ee**n
On **ea**ting m**ea**t that isn't l**ea**n,
I really f**ee**l that you should s**ee**
A dietician – which is m**e**!

Additional exercises:

A: *Write down 4 words with the target sound that you often use when speaking English. Practice these words, thinking about your lips, tongue and jaw positions for the target sound.*

1. _____   3. _____

2. _____   4. _____

B: *Write down 4 words with the target sound that you often hear on TV, radio or from your friends/colleagues. Practice these words, thinking about your lips, tongue and jaw positions for the target sound.*

1. _____   3. _____

2. _____   4. _____

Lesson 7: The [ɜʳ] sound as in "third"

Speech organs position:
Relaxed lips, jaw half-open
and the centre of the tongue
just slightly rising.
The tongue tip curls up
for the [r] sound.

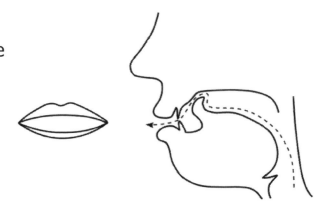

[ɜʳ   ɜʳ   ɜʳ]

A20
🎧 **Words**

Listen and repeat. Look at the mouth diagram to help you position your lips, tongue and jaw for the target sound.

Spelling variations for the [ɜʳ] sound	Highlighted bold letters pronounced as [ɜʳ]
er	p**er**jury, comm**er**cial, pres**er**ve, p**er**sonal
ir	sh**ir**t, f**ir**st, st**ir**, g**ir**l, S**ir**, b**ir**d, f**ir**m, fl**ir**t, b**ir**th
ear	y**ear**n, **ear**n, p**ear**l, **ear**ly
ur	occ**ur**, m**ur**muring, b**ur**den, b**ur**n, p**ur**pose, p**ur**se, c**ur**rent, c**ur**rency
or	w**or**k, w**or**se, w**or**ld, w**or**d

A21
🎧 **Sentences**

1. "The e**ar**ly b**ir**d catches the w**or**m." *(Proverb)*
2. Fl**ir**tatious g**ir**ls w**er**e **ur**ged not to dist**ur**b K**ur**t.
3. This p**ur**ple sh**ir**t is the w**or**st in the w**or**ld! I have no w**or**ds!
4. The g**ir**l h**ear**d that she came in th**ir**d in the W**or**ld Championships as a h**ur**dl**er**.
5. **Ur**sula obs**er**ved that the boy wore a d**ir**ty p**ur**ple sh**ir**t.
6. We w**er**e w**or**king in the W**or**ld Bank at f**ir**st; then we w**er**e transf**er**red to the Comm**er**cial Chambers in P**er**th.
7. My boyfriend is a p**er**fect n**er**d who makes his **ear**ning when everyone else is y**ear**ning.

A22
🎧 **Verses**

Listen and copy the intonation and voice modulation on the AUDIO TRACKS.

When I was young I s**er**ved a t**er**m
As office boy to an att**or**ney's f**ir**m.
The rich att**or**ney was good as his w**or**d;
And every day my voice was h**ear**d.

You're far too strict and very st**er**n,
Your views are always very f**ir**m,
You've heard of the proverb "the w**or**m will t**ur**n",
Now is your chance to live and l**ea**rn!

Additional exercises:

A: *Write down 4 words with the target sound that you often use when speaking English. Practice these words, thinking about your lips, tongue and jaw positions for the target sound.*

1. _____   3. _____

2. _____   4. _____

B: *Write down 4 words with the target sound that you often hear on TV, radio or from your friends/colleagues. Practice these words, thinking about your lips, tongue and jaw positions for the target sound.*

1. _____   3. _____

2. _____   4. _____

Lesson 8: The [ə] neutral vowel (schwa) as in "the"

Speech organs position:
Jaw is half-open, relaxed lips; the middle of the tongue rises slightly. The sound is very short and always appears in unstressed syllables.

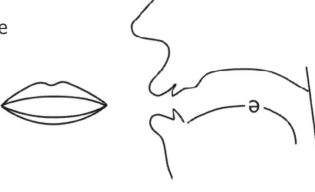

[ə   ə   ə]

A23
🎧 **Words**

	Highlighted bold letters pronounced as [ə]
The first syllable unstressed	**a**way, **a**gree, **a**buse, **a**board, **a**gainst, **a**ttain, c**a**nal, c**o**rrect, p**o**lice, **o**bserve, s**u**ppose, s**u**pport, s**u**pply, s**u**rround
The second syllable unstressed	abs**e**nt, const**a**nt, or**a**l, devel**o**ped, dipl**o**mat, giv**e**n, sev**e**n, doz**e**n, fed**e**ral, inst**a**nce, discuss**io**n, confus**io**n, intuit**io**n, permiss**io**n,

A24
🎧 **Unstressed positions**

and	**a**	**an**
Black **and** white	Get **a** spoon	Have **an** apple
Pork **and** beans	Cut **a** piece	**A** question and **an** answer
Ladies **and** gentlemen	Here's **a** plate	**A**n aunt and **an** uncle
	Lend **a** hand	Listen to **an** announcement

NB: Schwa is the most-used sound in English. Very often, unstressed syllables and words in a sentence are pronounced with a schwa.

A25
🎧 Sentences

Listen and repeat. Read each sentence aloud slowly at first, then as if you were telling it to someone in a natural way.

1. Is it made **of** glass? No, it's made **of** plastic.
2. What c**a**n I do? What h**a**s she done? What h**a**ve you done?
3. The c**o**nductor of the orchestr**a** w**a**s **a**mazed to see th**e** viol**a** player drink **a** scotch **and** sod**a**.
4. Tell **A**mand**a** to buy some b**a**nan**a**s **a**s well **a**s p**o**tatoes **and** t**o**matoes.

A26
🎧 Comparison: stressed and unstressed vowel position

Stressed position	Unstressed position, pronounced with [ə]
What are you looking **a**t? [æ]	Look **a**t him!
What is it made **o**f? [ɒ]	It's made **of** cotton.
Where do you come fr**o**m? [ɒ]	I come fr**o**m Paris.
W**a**sn't he there? [ʊ]	Yes, he w**a**s sitting next to me.

A27
🎧 Verses

Listen and copy the intonation and voice modulation on the AUDIO TRACKS.

My jeal**ou**sy I can't express,
Their love they **o**p**e**nly c**o**nfess;
Her shell-like ears she does not close
T**o** their recit**a**l **of** their woes.

Lesson 9: The coloured schwa [ər] sound as in "doctor"

Speech organs position:
Relaxed lips, jaw half-open and the centre of the tongue just slightly rising; the tongue tip curls up to the [r] position.

[ər   ər   ər]

A28
🎧 Words

Listen and repeat. Look at the mouth diagram to help you position your lips, tongue and jaw for the target sound.

Spelling variations for the [3ʳ] sound	Highlighted bold letters pronounced as [3ʳ]
ure	cul**ture**, fig**ure**, sculp**ture**, fea**ture**, trea**sure**,
or	tut**or**, doct**or**, eff**or**t, collect**or**, fav**or**, debt**or**,
ar, er, re	forw**ar**d, upw**ar**d, awkw**ar**d, famili**ar**, stand**ar**d, lead**er**, spend**er**, lov**er**, cent**er**, theat**er**

A29
🎧 Sentences

1. I fig**ure** that the found**er** of Microsoft is a numb**er** one comput**er** nerd.
2. Gold-digg**er** Esth**er** fav**or**s lawy**er**s and bank**er**s to teach**er**s and farm**er**s.
3. Our yoga teach**er** shows us how to stretch upw**ar**d and forw**ar**d and monit**or**s our progress.
4. Doct**or** Sandl**er** made a herculean eff**or**t to help my sist**er** Hest**er**.

A30
🎧 Verses
I nev**er** drive a big, big car!
What nev**er**?
No, nev**er**!
What, nev**er**?
Well, hardly ev**er**!

An orphan boy called Pet**er** Glov**er**,
Always wanted to find his moth**er**,
Oh joy of joys he did discov**er**
He found he had anoth**er** broth**er**!

Classes of words that have the neutral vowel shwa [ə]

1. Endings of names: **A**mand**a**, Barbar**a**, Olg**a**, S**a**manth**a**, Arth**ur**.

2. Names of places ending in "mouth" will usually have [ə] after "m": Bournem**ou**th, Exm**ou**th, Dartm**ou**th, Portsm**ou**th, Plym**ou**th.

3. Contraction of "have" to [əv]: could**'ve**, should**'ve**, must**'ve**, might**'ve**.

4. Auxiliary verbs in unstressed position will often have [ə]: h**a**ve, h**a**s, h**a**d

5. Articles, prepositions and particles in unstressed position will often have [ə]: **a**, th**e**, t**o**, **o**f, **a**s, fr**o**m.

Additional exercises:

A: *Write down 4 words with the target sound that you often use when speaking English. Practice these words, thinking about your lips, tongue and jaw positions for the target sound.*

1. _____ 3. _____

2. _____ 4. _____

B: *Write down 4 words with the target sound that you often hear on TV, radio or from your friends/colleagues. Practice these words, thinking about your lips, tongue and jaw positions for the target sound.*

1. _____ 3. _____

2. _____ 4. _____

Lesson 10: The [ɪ] sound as in "pit"

Speech organs position:
Jaw is nearly closed, lips slightly spread; the front of the tongue rises high in the front of the mouth.

[ɪ   ɪ   ɪ]

A31
🎧 **Words**

Spelling variations for the [ɪ] sound	Highlighted bold letters pronounced as [ɪ]
i	h**i**m, h**i**larious, h**i**deous, h**i**nt, wh**i**m, v**i**sion, sp**i**r**i**t
a	vill**a**ge, cribb**a**ge
e	d**e**lete, d**e**feat, d**e**lusion
y	s**y**mbol, s**y**mptoms, h**y**mn

A32
🎧 **Sentences**

1. Bill tentatively lifted the lid of the bin and found not a single thing.
2. Tell Jill I think this is a silly little game.
3. I can't stay a minute longer in this miserable little pit!
4. Tim Grim is a solid, respectable man who is a pillar of society.
5. This simple thing, a wedding ring, is a symbol, the oldest in history.

🎧 **Verses**

Here's a first–rate opportunity
To get married with **i**mpunity,
To **i**ndulge **i**n the fel**i**c**i**ty
Of unbounded domest**i**c**i**ty.
You shall qu**i**ckly be personnified,
Conjugally matr**i**monnified,
By a doctor of d**i**v**i**nity,
Who resides **i**n th**i**s v**i**c**i**nity.

Additional exercises:

A: *Write down 4 words with the target sound that you often use when speaking English. Practice these words, thinking about your lips, tongue and jaw positions for the target sound.*

1. _____   3. _____

2. _____   4. _____

B: *Write down 4 words with the target sound that you often hear on TV, radio or from your friends/colleagues. Practice these words, thinking about your lips, tongue and jaw positions for the target sound.*

1. _____   3. _____

2. _____   4. _____

Lesson 11: Comparison [ə] - [ɪ] and [ɪ] - [i]

A34

🎧 **Comparison: [i] as in "please" and short [ɪ] as in "pit"**

[ɪ]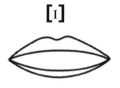

[i]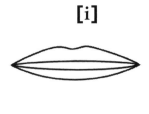

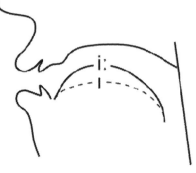

[i]	[ɪ]	[i]	[ɪ]
reason	risen	beast	bit
ease	is	deal	dill
sleep	slip	greed	grid
cheap	chip	leave	live
wheat	wit	sneaky	snip
leap	lip	beat	bit
feet	fit	deed	did
team	Tim	green	grin
eat	it	heel	hill
keys	kiss	creep	crypt
feel	fill	neat	nit
heat	hit	reed	rid
jeep	Jill	seek	sick
meal	mill	steal	still
peel	pill	thief	thing
these	this	weep	whip
sheep	ship	cheek	chick

A35

32

🎧 Words: [i] highlighted as bold and underlined and [ɪ] highlighted as bold

def**ea**t	sn**ee**zing	m**ee**ting
rec**e**de	th**e**sis	y**ie**lding
retr**ie**ve	s**ee**ing	s**ei**zing
rec**ei**pt	ser**e**ne	fr**ee**zing

A36

🎧 Sentences: [ɪ] highlighted as bold and [i] highlighted as bold and underlined

1. The w**i**dth of the sl**ee**ves still n**ee**ds to fit my n**ea**t linen jacket.
2. I am not particularly k**ee**n to give the victory to a different t**ea**m.
3. T**i**m **i**s compl**e**tely out of N**i**na's l**ea**gue and sh**e** **i**sn't k**ee**n on b**ei**ng chased by h**i**m.
4. There **i**s a l**i**ttle someth**i**ng m**i**ssing **i**n th**i**s m**ea**l. Have you tried to add some dill?
5. My next of k**i**n, M**i**ster B**ea**n, **i**s a D**ea**n of **I**llinois Univers**i**t**y**.

A37
🎧 Verses

It **i**s exc**ee**dingly n**ea**t!
I fanc**y** that that w**i**ll do.
It **i**s certainl**y** ver**y** compl**e**te.
Ing**e**nious! Splendid, Sue!

Lesson 12: The [ʌ] sound as in "duck"

Speech organs position:
Jaw is half-open, relaxed
lips; the middle of the tongue
rises slightly. The sound
is very short.

[ʌ   ʌ   ʌ]

A38
🎧 Words

Spelling variations for the [ʌ] sound	Highlighted bold letters pronounced as [ʌ]
u	m**u**st, l**u**ck, d**u**mp, j**u**st, **u**pper, n**u**n, b**u**s, l**u**nch
o	c**o**me, fr**o**nt, l**o**ve, d**o**ne, **o**nce, c**o**ver
ou	r**ou**gh, t**ou**gh, c**ou**ntry, c**ou**ple, d**ou**ble, tr**ou**ble

A39
🎧 Sentences

1. For s**o**me**o**ne with a l**o**ve of m**o**ney, the s**u**m of **o**ne h**u**ndred dollars was enticing.
2. B**u**d, l**o**ve! Don't give **u**p; victory is in fr**o**nt of you!
3. I can't **u**nderstand the f**u**n of travelling by b**u**s on such r**ou**gh c**ou**ntry roads.
4. There are a n**u**mber of n**u**ns am**o**ng **u**s.
5. Here I am, in fr**o**nt of a t**u**b with a r**u**b and a scr**u**b!
6. When you c**o**me to l**u**nch on S**u**nday, remember to bring s**o**me m**o**ney.

A40
🎧 **Verses**

My peas I eat with r**u**nny h**o**ney,
I've d**o**ne so all my life,
I know it d**oe**s taste rather f**u**nny,
But it keeps them on the knife!

A chocolate b**u**n is a lot of f**u**n,
But you will not have m**u**ch l**u**ck
With a cr**u**nchy n**u**t!

Additional exercises:

A: *Write down 4 words with the target sound that you often use when speaking English. Practice these words, thinking about your lips, tongue and jaw positions for the target sound.*

1. _____ 3. _____

2. _____ 4. _____

B: *Write down 4 words with the target sound that you often hear on TV, radio or from your friends/colleagues. Practice these words, thinking about your lips, tongue and jaw positions for the target sound.*

1. _____ 3. _____

2. _____ 4. _____

Lesson 13: The [ɛ] sound as in "pen"

Speech organs position:
Jaw is half open, lips are
in a soft smile position;
the front of the tongue rises
three quarters of the way
up towards the roof of the
mouth.

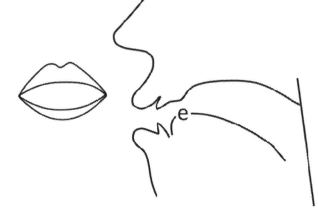

[ɛ   ɛ   ɛ]

A41
🎧 Words

Listen and repeat. Look at the mouth diagram to help you position your lips, tongue and jaw for the target sound.

Spelling variations for the [ɛ] sound	Highlighted bold letters pronounced as [ɛ]
e	sensible, beg, bent, generosity, technically
eo	leopard, jeopardy
ea	head, wealth, measure, pleasure, thread,
ei, ai	friend, said
ay	says

A42
🎧 **Comparison:** [ə] and [ɛ]

[ə]	[ɛ]
canal	kennel
correct	kept
gazette	geld
police	pet
support	self-help
command	ketchup
American	embassy

A43
🎧 Sentences

1. "It's b**e**st for your p**e**t's h**ea**lth to r**e**st", s**ai**d an **e**ducated v**e**t to a w**ea**lthy g**e**ntlemen.
2. **E**ducated m**e**n have always m**ea**sured **e**very word they s**ai**d.
3. Tw**e**nty-s**e**ven sh**e**pherds h**e**sitated before **e**ntering the p**e**n.
4. A r**e**d l**ea**ther jacket was w**e**ll pres**e**nted on the display.
5. The w**ea**ther was w**e**t and windy wh**e**n the m**e**n were m**e**nding the f**e**nce.

A44
🎧 Verses

Listen and copy the intonation and voice modulation on the AUDIO TRACKS.

Every moment brings a tr**ea**sure,
Of its own esp**e**cial pl**ea**sure...
L**e**t us gaily tr**ea**d the m**ea**sure.

Additional exercises:

A: *Write down 4 words with the target sound that you often use when speaking English. Practice these words, thinking about your lips, tongue and jaw positions for the target sound.*

1. _____ 3. _____

2. _____ 4. _____

B: *Write down 4 words with the target sound that you often hear on TV, radio or from your friends/colleagues. Practice these words, thinking about your lips, tongue and jaw positions for the target sound.*

1. _____ 3. _____

2. _____ 4. _____

Lesson 14: Vowel [ɛʳ] as in "care"

Speech organs position:

Start with the vowel [ɛ] as
in "pet": the jaw is half open, the lips
spread, the front of the tongue rising
to about three quarters of the way
up.
The tongue tip curls up to the [r]
position.

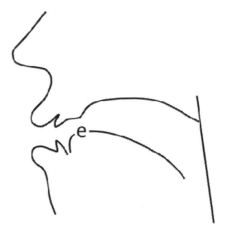

[ɛ ɛ ɛʳ   ɛ ɛ ɛʳ ɛʳ ɛʳ ɛʳ]

A45
🎧 **Words**

Spelling variations for the [eə] sound	Highlighted bold letters pronounced as [eə]
air	rep**air**, f**air**y, desp**air**, fl**air**, p**ear**
a before **r**	prec**ar**ious, sc**ar**cely, vic**ar**ious, nef**ar**ious, c**a**re
are	sc**are**, squ**are**, comp**are**, bew**are**, gl**are**

A46
🎧 **Sentences**

1. Please, take c**are** of our h**eir**! But bew**are**, he can be unb**ea**rable.
2. I comp**are**d my questionn**aire** with Cl**are**'s and fell into desp**air** as I became aw**are** that my questionn**aire** was rather b**are**.
3. I cannot d**are**, nor can I b**ear**, an aff**air** with a married man.
4. I like to w**ear** my h**air** groomed with c**are**.
5. I'm prep**are**d to sw**ear** that the sh**er**iff r**are**ly sh**are**d a h**are**.
6. Take c**are**! These ch**air**s have had th**eir** f**air** sh**are** of w**ear** and t**ear**.

A47

Listen and copy the intonation and voice modulation on the AUDIO TRACKS.

Cl**are** arrived with the Sh**er**iff,
With beautiful silver shoes to w**ear**,
With her usual haughty st**are**,
And her nose up in the **air**!

Additional exercises:

A: *Write down 4 words with the target sound that you often use when speaking English. Practice these words, thinking about your lips, tongue and jaw positions for the target sound.*

1. _____   3. _____

2. _____   4. _____

B: *Write down 4 words with the target sound that you often hear on TV, radio or from your friends/colleagues. Practice these words, thinking about your lips, tongue and jaw positions for the target sound.*

1. _____   3. _____

2. _____   4. _____

Lesson 15: The [ʊ] sound as in "book"

Speech organs position:

The jaw is almost closed,
lips rounded and forward.
The back of the tongue is high
in the back of the mouth.

[ʊ   ʊ   ʊ]

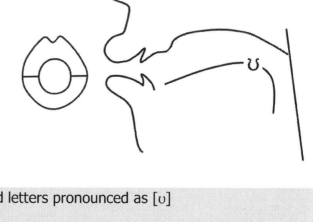

A48

🎧 **Words**

Spelling variations for the [ʊ] sound	Highlighted bold letters pronounced as [ʊ]
u	p**u**sh, f**u**ll, b**u**tcher, spoonf**u**l, f**u**lfil, c**u**shion, s**u**gar
oo, o	b**oo**k, l**oo**k, g**oo**d, w**oo**l, w**oo**d, w**o**lf, f**oo**t, st**oo**d
oul	c**ou**ld, w**ou**ld, sh**ou**ld

A49

🎧 **Sentences**

1. C**ou**ld you p**u**t this g**oo**d w**oo**l in the w**oo**den chest?
2. The b**u**tcher saw a w**o**lf l**oo**king in every n**oo**k for the fallen r**oo**k.
3. Our c**oo**k c**ou**ldn't c**oo**k without l**oo**king at his c**oo**kb**oo**k.
4. If I c**ou**ld just get off the h**oo**k and get rid of my responsibility to c**oo**k.
5. You c**ou**ld easily lose your f**oo**ting in the b**u**lrushes by the br**oo**k.

A50
🎧 **Verses**

Would you take this book?
Could you leave that hook?
Let us walk by foot!
That sounds good!
We could, we would, we should!

Additional exercises:

A: *Write down 4 words with the target sound that you often use when speaking English. Practice these words, thinking about your lips, tongue and jaw positions for the target sound.*

1. _____   3. _____

2. _____   4. _____

B: *Write down 4 words with the target sound that you often hear on TV, radio or from your friends/colleagues. Practice these words, thinking about your lips, tongue and jaw positions for the target sound.*

1. _____   3. _____

2. _____   4. _____

Lesson 16: Vowels [ʊʳ] as in "poor"

Speech organs position:
Start with lips forward like
for the short vowel [ʊ]
as in "book" (Lesson 13),
Then curl up the tongue tip
into
the [r] position.

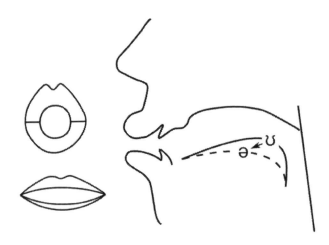

[ʊ ʊ ʊʳ   ʊ ʊ ʊʳ ʊʳ ʊʳ ʊʳ]

A51
🎧 Words

Spelling variations for the [ʊʳ] sound	Highlighted bold letters pronounced as [ʊʳ]
or	p**oor**, m**oor**, t**our**, d**our**, ins**ure**, r**ur**al, ass**ure**
ur	pl**ur**al, l**ur**e
for the [jʊʳ] sound	
ure	p**ure**, mat**ure**, obsc**ure**

A52
🎧 Sentences

1. The immat**ur**e jury was uns**ur**e and could no longer end**ur**e sp**ur**ious ass**ur**ances.
2. Obsc**ur**e r**ur**al m**oor**s all**ur**e M**ur**iel more than lux**ur**ious t**our**s.
3. D**our** Mr. R**uh**r was end**ur**ing the c**ur**e after his fiasco in am**our**.
4. The p**ur**e girl was l**ur**ed into the woods by f**ur**ious St**uar**t.
5. I ass**ur**e you, the r**ur**al Yorkshire m**oor**s are worth visiting on the t**our** of E**ur**ope.

A53
🎧 Verses

False is he whose vows all**ur**ing
Make the listening echoes ring;
Sweet and low when all-end**ur**ing
Are the songs the lovers sing!

Additional exercises:

A: *Write down 4 words with the target sound that you often use when speaking English. Practice these words, thinking about your lips, tongue and jaw positions for the target sound.*

1. _____ 3. _____

2. _____ 4. _____

B: *Write down 4 words with the target sound that you often hear on TV, radio or from your friends/colleagues. Practice these words, thinking about your lips, tongue and jaw positions for the target sound.*

1. _____ 3. _____

2. _____ 4. _____

Lesson 17: Comparison [ʊ] and [u]

A54

🎧 Contrast between [ʊ] as in "book"·
and [u] as in "beauty"

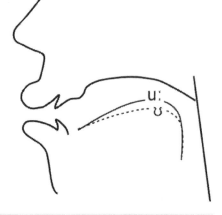

[ʊ]	[u]	[ʊ]	[u]
could	clue	good	glued
foot	food	wood	wound
full	fruit	book	boom
look	loose	took	true
put	pool	rook	rouge
should	shoes	soot	soon

A55

🎧 **Sentences: short [ʊ] sound highlighted as bold and long [u:] highlighted as black and underlined**

1. The **wou**nded w**o**lf c**ou**ldn't m**o**ve his **foo**t and <u>soo</u>n fell asleep under the b**u**sh.
2. This g**oo**d w**oo**l w**ou**ld b<u>eau</u>tifully s<u>ui</u>t my n<u>ew</u> bl<u>ue</u> s<u>ui</u>t.
3. Natural f**oo**ds contrib<u>u</u>te to a g**oo**d diet.
4. Behaving l<u>oo</u>sely c**ou**ld be seen as f**oo**lish and w**ou**ldn't impr**o**ve your l**oo**ks.
5. G**oo**d b**oo**ks <u>u</u>sually f**u**lfil people's lives.

44

Additional exercises:

A: *Write down 4 words with the target sound that you often use when speaking English. Practice these words, thinking about your lips, tongue and jaw positions for the target sound.*

1. _____   3. _____

2. _____   4. _____

B: *Write down 4 words with the target sound that you often hear on TV, radio or from your friends/colleagues. Practice these words, thinking about your lips, tongue and jaw positions for the target sound.*

1. _____   3. _____

2. _____   4. _____

Lesson 18: The [æ] sound as in "cat"

Speech organs position:
Open jaw, open loose lips; tongue almost flat at the bottom of the mouth.
The sound is made in the front of the mouth.

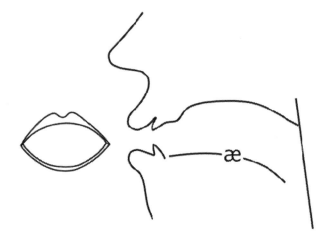

[æ   æ   æ]

A56
🎧 **Words**

> **a**ctivity, apparent, **a**ccent, **a**ctually, **a**nswer, **a**sk, br**a**nch, diplom**a**t, dem**a**nd, dis**a**ster, ex**a**mple, f**a**st, gl**a**ss, gr**a**nt, gr**a**sp, gr**a**ss, h**a**lf, m**a**ster, n**a**sty, p**a**th, pr**a**ctice, s**a**mple, staff, t**a**sk

A57
🎧 **Comparison: [e] and [æ] sounds**

[e]	[æ]	[e]	[æ]
fed	fad	ten	tan
head	hand	said	sad
leapt	lapped	breath	bandage
led	lad	kettle	cattle
bet	bat	set	sat
red	radical	head	had
bed	bad	message	manage
hen	hand	dead	dad
leg	lag	hem	ham
Ben	ban	lend	land
send	sand	vet	vat
tempo	Tampa	pen	pan
slept	slapped	kept	capped

A58
🎧 **Sentences**

1. A black fat cat was sad when he couldn't grab a slice of ham.
2. It can be quite a challenge to manage a marriage.
3. A man who looked unhappy badly sang a sad mad romantic song.
4. As a habit I add some tomato to my hamburger.
5. Standing hand in hand, the man asked Jan for her hand in marriage.
6. Can you manage to carry those magazines back to the rack?
7. I had to haggle over the price of hats.

A59
🎧 **Verses**

Paw of cat the chestnut snatches;
Worn-out garments show the patches;
Only count the chick that hatches
Men are grown-up catchy-catchies.

Additional exercises:

A: *Write down 4 words with the target sound that you often use when speaking English. Practice these words, thinking about your lips, tongue and jaw positions for the target sound.*

1. _____   3. _____

2. _____   4. _____

B: *Write down 4 words with the target sound that you often hear on TV, radio or from your friends/colleagues. Practice these words, thinking about your lips, tongue and jaw positions for the target sound.*

1. _____   3. _____

2. _____   4. _____

Lesson 19: Diphthong [oʊ] as in "home"

Speech organs position:
Start with a round lip
position [o], then
bring the lips forward into
[ʊ] as in "book" position.
The back of the tongue
moves from ¾ up into higher
position.

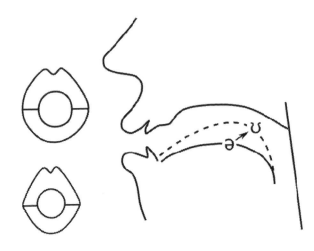

[o o oʊ   o o oʊ   oʊ oʊ oʊ]

A60
🎧 **Words**

Spelling variations for the [əʊ] sound	Highlighted bold letters pronounced as [əʊ]
o	h**o**pe, r**o**le, f**o**cus, th**o**se, b**o**th, cl**o**thes, **o**pen
oa	r**oa**d, **oa**k, c**oa**t
ow	gl**ow**, sorr**ow**, pill**ow**, foll**ow**, sparr**ow**, thr**ow**
ew	s**ew**

A61
🎧 **Sentences**

1. J**oa**n has a runny n**o**se because she r**o**de her p**o**ny through the fr**o**zen sn**ow**.
2. The inappr**o**priate language of the p**o**ems imp**o**sed a strange t**o**ne on the sh**ow**.
3. I d**o**n't kn**ow** when I will come h**o**me, alth**ou**gh I am cl**o**sely f**o**cusing on the r**oa**d. But soon, m**o**st probably, I will kn**o**w and will ph**o**ne you as soon as I come cl**o**ser to our h**o**me.
4. J**oe**, g**o** to **O**klah**o**ma and **O**hi**o**, then come h**o**me to R**o**me.

🎧 **Verses**

Listen and copy the intonation and voice modulation on the AUDIO TRACKS.

M**o**ses supp**o**ses his t**oe**ses are r**o**ses,
But M**o**ses supp**o**ses err**o**neously;
For n**o**body's t**oe**ses are p**o**sies of r**o**ses
As M**o**ses supp**o**ses his t**oe**ses to be.

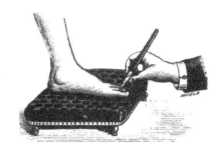

Additional exercises:

A: *Write down 4 words with the target sound that you often use when speaking English. Practice these words, thinking about your lips, tongue and jaw positions for the target sound.*

1. _____   3. _____

2. _____   4. _____

B: *Write down 4 words with the target sound that you often hear on TV, radio or from your friends/colleagues. Practice these words, thinking about your lips, tongue and jaw positions for the target sound.*

1. _____   3. _____

2. _____   4. _____

Lesson 20: Diphthong [eɪ] as in "cake"

Speech organs position:
Start in [e] as in "pet" position, with the lips in a soft smile and raised front of the tongue (Lesson 12).
Then the front of the tongue rises a little more forward, to [ɪ] as in "pit" position, and the lips spread slightly (Lesson 7).

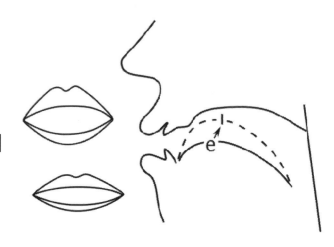

[e e eɪ   e e eɪ   eɪ eɪ eɪ]

A63
🎧 **Words**

Spelling variations for the [eɪ] sound	Highlighted bold letters pronounced as [eɪ]
a	t**a**ke, arr**a**nge, l**a**te, t**a**pe, am**a**ze, ch**a**nge, sh**a**pe, f**a**vor, s**a**ving, **a**gency, p**a**tience, compl**ai**nt
ea	br**ea**k, gr**ea**t
ai	**ai**m, r**ai**nbow, v**ai**n, g**ai**n, pl**ai**n, r**ai**n, tr**ai**n, m**ai**l
ay	g**ay**, tr**ay**, betr**ay**, p**ay**ment, del**ay**, ok**ay**
eigh, aigh	w**eigh**t, **eigh**t, str**aigh**t

A64
🎧 **Sentences**

1. The tr**ai**n at **eigh**t was very l**a**te; we left the st**a**tion with frustr**a**tion.
2. We p**a**tiently w**ai**ted in v**ai**n for our f**a**vorite t**a**ble to become v**a**cant.
3. Some m**ay** consider it ins**a**ne to n**a**me a child with an **a**ncient n**a**me!
4. All the f**a**vorite c**a**kes that J**a**ne had m**a**de were pl**a**ced on tr**ay**s.
5. You must p**ay** any d**ay** if you are going aw**ay** on the tr**ai**n.

A65

🎧 **Verses**

Instructions: Copy the intonation and modulate the voice after the AUDIO TRACKS.

The rain in Spain stays mainly on the plain.
The plains in Spain are mainly full of rain.

Additional exercises:

A: *Write down 4 words with the target sound that you often use when speaking English. Practice these words, thinking about your lips, tongue and jaw positions for the target sound.*

1. _____   3. _____

2. _____   4. _____

B: *Write down 4 words with the target sound that you often hear on TV, radio or from your friends/colleagues. Practice these words, thinking about your lips, tongue and jaw positions for the target sound.*

1. _____   3. _____

2. _____   4. _____

Lesson 21: Diphthong [ɔɪ] as in "boy"

Speech organs position:
Starting with a long [ɔ] sound as in "caught" (Lesson 3), with the lips forward and quite tight. The jaw is fairly closed, the lips relaxed. Then move to [ɪ] as in "pit" position, Lesson 10; the tongue rises forward, lips slightly spread.

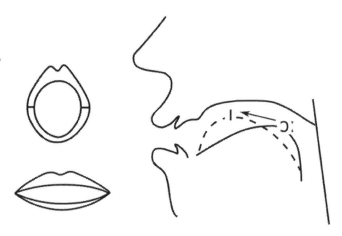

[ɔɪ ɔɪ ɔɪ   ɔ ɔ ɔɪ   ɔɪ ɔɪ ɔɪ]

A66
🎧 **Words**

Spelling variations for the [ɔɪ] sound	Highlighted bold letters pronounced as [ɔɪ]
oi	c**oi**n, expl**oi**t, m**oi**sture, b**oi**l, sp**oi**l, p**oi**se, an**oi**nt, s**oi**l, p**oi**nts, br**oi**l, f**oi**l, l**oi**ter, inv**oi**ce
oy	enj**oy**, l**oy**al, ann**oy**, r**oy**al, t**oy**, dec**oy**, destr**oy**

A67
🎧 **Sentences**

1. Tr**oy** was once destr**oy**ed by flamb**oy**ant n**oi**sy soldiers.
2. When it came to choosing t**oy**s, J**oy** Ll**oy**d was sp**oi**led for ch**oi**ce.
3. Rice requires m**oi**st s**oi**l and months of t**oi**l.
4. Any n**oi**se ann**oy**s an **oy**ster, but a n**oi**sy n**oi**se ann**oy**s an **oy**ster most.
5. You can't enj**oy** the beef if the j**oi**nt is covered with b**oi**ling **oi**l.
6. M**oi**ra was very ann**oy**ed at the b**oi**sterous n**oi**se of her b**oy**-t**oy** enj**oy**ing his **oy**sters.

🎧 **Verses**

Little R**oy** was a very sp**oi**led b**oy**,
With a talent to ann**oy**,
The quickest way to stop his n**oi**se
Was to take away his t**oy**s.

Additional exercises:

A: *Write down 4 words with the target sound that you often use when speaking English. Practice these words, thinking about your lips, tongue and jaw positions for the target sound.*

1. _____ 3. _____

2. _____ 4. _____

B: *Write down 4 words with the target sound that you often hear on TV, radio or from your friends/colleagues. Practice these words, thinking about your lips, tongue and jaw positions for the target sound.*

1. _____ 3. _____

2. _____ 4. _____

Lesson 22: Diphthong [iə] as in "theatre" and [iəʳ] as in "dear" ʳ

Speech organs position:
Starting with a long [i] position as in "peat", then dropping the tongue back into the schwa [ə]. Add [r] and you get [iəʳ]

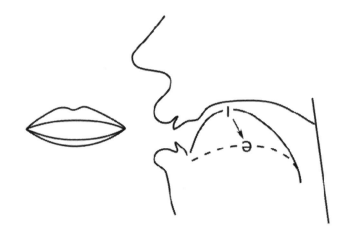

[i i iə   i i iə   iə iə iə]

A69
🎧 **Words**

Spelling variations for the [iə] sound	Highlighted bold letters pronounced as [iə]
ea	cer**ea**l, th**ea**ter
ie, ia	exper**ie**nce, immed**ia**tely, inconven**ie**nt
iou	myster**iou**s, cur**iou**s, spur**iou**s

Spelling variations for the [iəʳ] sound ʳ	Highlighted bold letters pronounced as [iəʳ]
ear	nucl**ear**, g**ear**, n**ear**ly, d**ear**, h**ear**, b**ear**d, f**ear**
ier	b**ier**, p**ier**, caval**ier**
ei	w**ei**rd, w**ei**r
er	sph**er**e, interf**er**e, h**er**e, p**eer**, sh**eer**
io	super**io**r, exter**io**r

A70
🎧 **Sentences**

1. R**ea**lly cl**ear** b**eer** makes me ch**eer**ful but spur**iou**s b**eer** makes me fur**iou**s.
2. L**eah** d**ear**, wipe your t**ear**s, come h**ere** and sit n**ear** me!
3. My exper**ie**nce of p**ier**cing V**era**'s **ear**s was rather w**ei**rd.
4. Last **yea**r I had a delir**io**us exper**ie**nce when I was allowed to st**eer** the boat n**ear** the w**eir**.

54

5. My **tear**fulness soon cl**ear**ed when I met the d**ear**, **fear**less, myster**iou**s stranger.

A71
🎧 **Verses**

At first it app**ea**red
That I was a good engin**eer**,
But my p**eer**s interf**ere**d,
And made it very cl**ear**,
That I should become an auction**eer**.

Additional exercises:

A: *Write down 4 words with the target sound that you often use when speaking English. Practice these words, thinking about your lips, tongue and jaw positions for the target sound.*

1. _____ 3. _____

2. _____ 4. _____

B: *Write down 4 words with the target sound that you often hear on TV, radio or from your friends/colleagues. Practice these words, thinking about your lips, tongue and jaw positions for the target sound.*

1. _____ 3. _____

2. _____ 4. _____

Lesson 23: Diphthong [aɪ] as in "bride"

Speech organs position:
Starting with an open [a] sound, flat tongue, open jaw, then moving to [ɪ] as in "pit", the jaw closes and the tongue rises for the second part of the sound.

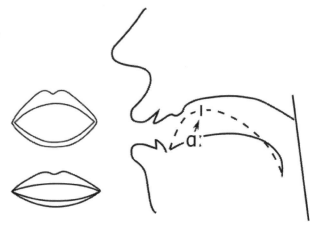

[a a aɪ   a a aɪ   aɪ aɪ aɪ]

A72
🎧 **Words**

Spelling variations for the [aɪ] sound	Highlighted bold letters pronounced as [aɪ]
y	sk**y**, fl**y**, cr**y**, suppl**y**, terrif**y**, den**y**, repl**y**
i	**i**dle, sl**i**de, sh**i**ne, w**i**ld, m**i**nd, sh**i**ne
igh, ui	h**igh**, n**igh**, g**ui**de

A73
🎧 **Sentences**

1. Tr**y** to find a w**i**se **i**dea beh**i**nd the rh**y**mes of Oscar W**i**lde.
2. The sun is no longer h**igh** in the sk**y** as the day decl**i**nes.
3. "His br**i**de is m**i**ld and k**i**nd." What? Are you bl**i**nd?
4. I know a few w**i**ld g**uy**s who have up to seven w**i**ves.
5. N**i**ne men with f**i**ne tenor voices dec**i**ded to sing h**igh** in the choir on Fr**i**day n**igh**t.

🎧 **Verses**

There was a lady loved a sw**i**ne,
She k**i**ndly asked:
Pig-hog will you be m**i**ne?
I will build you a silver st**y**,
In which you would **i**dly l**ie**.

Additional exercises:

A: *Write down 4 words with the target sound that you often use when speaking English. Practice these words, thinking about your lips, tongue and jaw positions for the target sound.*

1. _____   3. _____

2. _____   4. _____

B: *Write down 4 words with the target sound that you often hear on TV, radio or from your friends/colleagues. Practice these words, thinking about your lips, tongue and jaw positions for the target sound.*

1. _____   3. _____

2. _____   4. _____

Lesson 24: Diphthong [aʊ] as in "cow"

Speech organs position:
Start with flat tongue, open jaw in [a] position as in "pasta". Then bring the lips forward into the short [ʊ] position as in "book" (Lesson 13).

[a a aʊ   a a aʊ   aʊ aʊ aʊ]

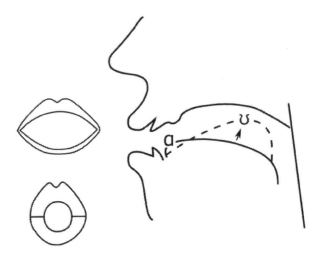

A75
🎧 **Words**

Spelling variations for the [aʊ] sound	Highlighted bold letters pronounced as [aʊ]
ou	f**ou**nd, m**ou**se, spr**ou**t, b**ou**nce, sh**ou**t, l**ou**d, d**ou**bt, sc**ou**t, m**ou**ntain, th**ou**sand, f**ou**ntain
ow	pr**ow**, tr**ow**el, v**ow**el, **ow**l, n**ow**, end**ow**, fl**ow**er

A76
🎧 **Sentences**

1. No d**ou**bt we can find th**ou**sands of fl**ow**ers in the m**ou**ntains of the S**ou**th.
2. H**ow** n**ow** br**ow**n c**ow**.
3. I saw a cl**ow**n sh**ou**ting in the t**ow**n.
4. Here should lie the body of Jonathan P**ou**nd, who was last seen at sea and never f**ou**nd.
5. The l**ou**d s**ou**nd of the h**ou**nds conf**ou**nded the br**ow**n m**ou**se.
6. With a sh**ou**t, the boy f**ou**nd a th**ou**sand dollars **ou**tside of the t**ow**n.

🎧 **Verses**

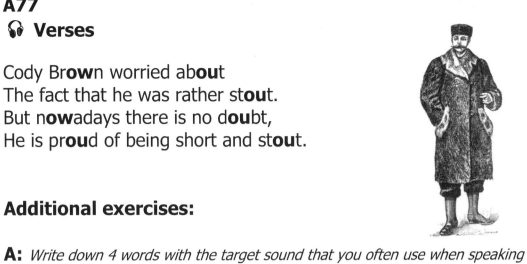

Cody Br**ow**n worried ab**ou**t
The fact that he was rather st**ou**t.
But n**ow**adays there is no d**ou**bt,
He is pr**ou**d of being short and st**ou**t.

Additional exercises:

A: *Write down 4 words with the target sound that you often use when speaking English. Practice these words, thinking about your lips, tongue and jaw positions for the target sound.*

1. _____   3. _____

2. _____   4. _____

B: *Write down 4 words with the target sound that you often hear on TV, radio or from your friends/colleagues. Practice these words, thinking about your lips, tongue and jaw positions for the target sound.*

1. _____   3. _____

2. _____   4. _____

Lesson 24: Semi-vowel [j] as in "yacht"

Semi-vowels are neither vowels nor consonants. The speech organs start as if you make a pure single vowel, but instead of making that sound, they immediately move to another sound.

Speech organs position:

Start with the front of the tongue high as in [iː] "feet"; then, immediately move the tongue down to the neutral [ə] schwa position.

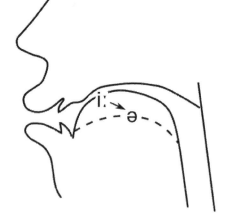

[j   j   j]

B1
🎧 Words

Spelling variations for the [j] sound	Highlighted bold letters pronounced as [j]
y	**y**oung, **y**es, **y**ou, **y**esterday, **y**ard, **y**arn
u	**u**se, arg**u**e, val**u**e, h**u**ge, ref**u**se, conf**u**se, **u**nisex
ew	n**ew**, f**ew**er

B2
🎧 Sentences

1. **Y**esterday, we were among the **few** to get a nice vi**ew**.
2. I was conf**u**sed that the bank ref**u**sed to accept **y**our **Eu**ros.
3. The **y**outh **y**elled out, "I **y**earn to go to N**ew** **Y**ork!"
4. **Y**ou kn**ew** **ye**sterday's n**ew**s about the **y**achts tour, didn't **y**ou?
5. In **U**nion Square, the sound of b**eau**tiful m**u**sic is not **u**nique.

B3

🎧 **Verses**

Listen and copy the intonation and voice modulation on the AUDIO TRACKS.

Love that no wrong can c**u**re,
Love that is always n**ew**,
Love that will aye end**u**re,
Though the rewards be f**ew**,
That is the love that's p**u**re,
That is the love that's true!

Additional exercises:

A: *Write down 4 words with the target sound that you often use when speaking English. Practice these words, thinking about your lips, tongue and jaw positions for the target sound.*

1. _____   3. _____

2. _____   4. _____

B: *Write down 4 words with the target sound that you often hear on TV, radio or from your friends/colleagues. Practice these words, thinking about your lips, tongue and jaw positions for the target sound.*

1. _____   3. _____

2. _____   4. _____

Lesson 25: Semi-vowel [w] as in "want"

Speech organs position:

Start with the lips forward, as in [uː] "boot", then immediately pull the lips back to the neutral [ə] schwa position.

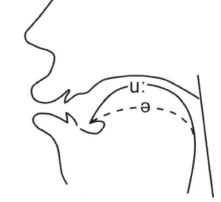

B4

🎧 **Repeat once from left to right:**

w	w	w	w
ww	ww	ww	w
www	www	www	w
wwww	wwww	wwww	w

B5

🎧 **Repeat each line four times:**

1. **W**ill you?
2. **W**ill you **w**ait?
3. **W**ill you **w**ait for **W**illy?
4. **W**ill you **w**ait for **W**illy and **W**innie?
5. **W**ill you **w**ait for **W**illy and **W**innie **W**illiams?

B6
🎧 Words

Spelling variations for the [w] sound	Highlighted bold letters pronounced as [w]
w	**w**ax, **w**olf, **w**ork, **w**ait, **w**ant, **w**atch, **w**eather
wh	**wh**ale, **wh**eel, **wh**ether
u after **q**	**qu**een, **qu**ench, **qu**antity
o	**o**nce, some**o**ne

B7
🎧 Words: contrasts with [v] and [w]

[v]	[w]	[v]	[w]
vet	**w**et	veal	**wh**eel
vest	**w**est	vend	**w**end
vale	**wh**ale	vent	**w**ent
vain	**w**ane	verse	**w**orse
via	**w**ire	vile	**wh**ile
vine	**w**ine	vim	**wh**im

B8
🎧 Sentences

1. **W**ill you be re**qu**ired to **w**ork in **W**ashington on **W**ednesdays?
2. I **w**ondered **wh**ether any **o**ne of you **w**ere **w**illing to ac**qui**re our ex**qui**site **w**ines.
3. The **qu**alitative results **w**ere not **w**hat **w**e **w**anted from our **qu**antifiable **qu**estionnaire **qu**estions.
4. Every**o**ne **w**ould **w**ant to have as a **w**ife a **w**ondrous **w**ise **w**oman **w**ith beautiful eyes.
5. He **w**on the a**w**ard for having **w**orn the **w**orld's **w**orst **w**aistcoat.

B9
🎧 Verses

We are blind, and **w**e **w**ould see;
We are bound, and **w**e **w**ould be free;
We are dumb, and **w**e **w**ould talk;
We are lame, and **w**e **w**ould **w**alk.

63

Lesson 26: Plosive consonants unvoiced [p] as in "pack" and voiced [b] as in "big"

When producing plosives the passage of the air is completely blocked by two speech organs coming together somewhere between the throat and the lips. Pressure is compressed behind them pushing the air. When the speech organs are suddenly released that trapped air which was completely pressed behind the blockage shoots out, and we hear a little explosion, that sound creates the consonant.

Speech organs position:

[p] and its partner [b] are made with the lips blocking the passage of the air. [p] is made purely with breath; [b] is made exactly the same way, but you vibrate the vocal chords to make a sound. If you block the passage of the air for a split second before you make [p], you can feel a little pressure behind the blockage and then you release it. Add voice to that explosion and you get [b]. Sharp, quick sounds.

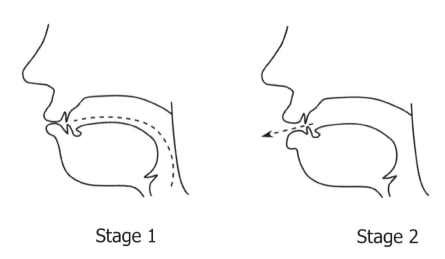

Stage 1   Stage 2

B10

🎧 **Repeat once from left to right:**

p	p	p	p
pp	pp	pp	p
ppp	ppp	ppp	p
pppp	pppp	pppp	p

64

B11
🎧 **Words for unvoiced [p] sound**

> **p**late, **p**lace, **p**antry, **p**arsley, **p**erform, **p**ublic, **p**resent, **p**rint, im**p**romptu, **p**leasant, **p**ersonal, **p**roperty, **p**re**c**i**p**itate

B12
🎧 **Sentences**

1. The **p**act on "**P**rivacy of **P**ersonal **P**roperty" was **p**rinted in the **p**aper.
2. He gave a **p**oor ex**p**lanation of the **p**ossibility of **p**ost**p**oning the **p**reliminary **p**lans to **p**ut a new **p**roduction manager in **p**lace.
3. **P**aul's **p**re**p**osterous im**p**romptu **p**erformance was **p**retty **p**ersonal and lacked **p**ro**p**riety.
4. **P**enelo**p**e **p**romoted a healthy **p**leasant a**pp**earance in her new s**p**ring com**p**ilation.
5. Although **p**izzas are **p**o**p**ular, most **p**eo**p**le **p**refer **p**retzels.
6. **P**ease **p**orridge hot, **p**ease **p**orridge cold, **p**ease **p**orridge in the **p**ot nine days old.

B13
🎧 **Tongue-twister**

Peter **P**i**p**er **p**icked a **p**eck of **p**ickled **p**e**pp**ers
A **p**eck of **p**ickled **p**e**pp**ers **P**eter **P**i**p**er **p**icked
If **P**eter **P**i**p**er **p**icked a **p**eck of **p**ickled **p**e**pp**ers
Where's the **p**eck of **p**ickled **p**e**pp**ers **P**eter **P**i**p**er **p**icked?

B14

🎧 **Articulation exercise**

A complicated gentleman allow me to present,
Of all the arts and faculties a terse
embodiment:
A great arithmetician, who can demonstrate
with ease,
That two and two are three or five, or
anything you please:
An eminent logician, who can make it clear to
you
That black is white – when looked at from the
proper point of view:
A marvellous philologist, who'll undertake to show,
That "yes" is but another form of "no".

B15

🎧 **Repeat once from left to right:**

b	b	b	b
bb	bb	bb	b
bbb	bbb	bbb	b
bbbb	bbbb	bbbb	b

B16

🎧 **Words for voiced [b]**

b	bring, baby, Bob, snob, bomb, balm
Nasal plosion	submit, submarine, sob noisily
Labial and lateral plosion	babble, trouble, table, double

B17

🎧 **Sentences**

1. Bill Bobby bought a big black cab and became a troubled driver.
2. The Bible on the table belonged to Barry Baker.
3. It was brilliant bursting bubbles in their billions during the ball in Boston.

66

4. **B**obb**y** and **B**renda saw a **b**lack **b**at and a **b**ig **b**umb**l**e **b**ee at a **b**ar**b**ecue with their neigh**b**ors.
5. The **b**lack**b**ird **b**uilt a **b**eautiful **b**ig nest.

B18
🎧 **Comparison: [p] and [b]**

[p]	[b]
pocket	**b**ucket
piece	**b**ees
pork	**b**ark
point	**b**oiled
panther	**b**ender
passport	**b**uzzword

B19
🎧 **Tongue-twister: the voiced [b] sound**

Betty **B**otter **b**ought some **b**utter,
But, she said the **b**utter's **b**itter;
If I put it in my **b**atter
It will make my **b**atter **b**itter,
But a **b**it of **b**etter **b**utter,
That would make my **b**atter **b**etter.

Additional exercises:

A: *Write down 4 words with the target sound that you often use when speaking English. Practice these words, thinking about your lips, tongue and jaw positions for the target sound.*

1. _____ 3. _____

B: *Write down 4 words with the target sound that you often hear on TV, radio or from your friends/colleagues. Practice these words, thinking about your lips, tongue and jaw positions for the target sound.*

1. _____ 3. _____

Lesson 27: Plosive consonants unvoiced [t] as in "talk", fast [d] as in "later" and silent "t" as in interest

Speech organs position:

Sounds are made with the tip of the tongue going up to the alveolar ridge, the gummed ridge behind the top teeth. There is a blockage for a split second; the tongue tip comes down sharply, the breath escapes and we get [t]. Add sound and we get [d].

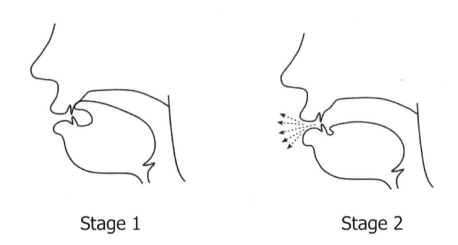

Stage 1   Stage 2

B20

🎧 **Repeat once from left to right:**

t	t	t	t
tt	tt	tt	t
ttt	ttt	ttt	t
tttt	tttt	tttt	t

B21

🎧 **Words: unvoiced [t] sound**

ten, tiny, try, turn, table, tennis, terrific, traffic, trend, transaction, electronic, stand, tremendous, trendy

B22

🎧 **Sentences: unvoiced [t] sound**

1. When playing table tennis, take turns every ten minutes.
2. Two toads totally tired of trying to trot to Tennessee.

3. **T**om researche**d** and **t**este**d** his **st**ate of the ar**t t**echnology **t**en **t**imes.
4. **It t**akes **t**wo **t**o **t**ango.

B23
🎧 **Verses**

Tricky **T**imothy **t**ook **t**wo **t**ies
To **t**ie **t**wo **t**ulips **t**o **t**wo **t**all **t**rees,
To **t**errify the **t**errible **Th**omas and **T**ullamees.

Fast [d]
In everyday speech Americans often use a fast [d]

B24
🎧 **Words:** [t] between vowels pronounced as fast [d] sound

tu**t**or, la**t**er, be**tt**er, li**ttl**e, ca**t**er, me**t**al, Bri**t**ish, fe**t**ish, shou**t**ing, wa**t**er, ma**tt**er, rou**t**ing, Pe**t**er, to**t**al, daugh**t**er, lo**tt**ery, puri**t**y

[t] between a vowel with "r" and a vowel pronounced as fast [d] sound

par**t**ed, car**t**er, for**t**y, thir**t**y, quar**t**er, spor**t**ing, star**t**ed, dir**t**ier, sor**t**ed, ver**t**igo

B25
🎧 **Phrases and sentences:**
[t] between words is pronounced as a fast [d] sound if it's between vowels

i**t** is, a**t** eight, ge**t** out, si**t** up, no**t** a**t** all, hi**t** it, ea**t** it, wri**t**e abou**t** it, wai**t** a second, pu**t** it out, wha**t** if, wha**t** about, pu**t** it away

1. Pe**t**er has to ge**t** up a**t** eight to look after his li**ttl**e daugh**t**er.
2. My **t**u**t**or told me to wri**t**e a be**tt**er le**tt**er.

69

Held [t] followed by [n] sound

When [t] is followed by [n], the [t] is not pronounced. The two vocal cords come together for a split second causing a blockage of the air passage. Then the tip of the tongue rises to the alveolar ridge to make the [n] sound, and the breath escapes through the nose.

B26
🎧 Words

| tn | mut**ton**, cot**ton**, but**ton**, ea**ten**, sen**ten**ce, threa**ten**, kit**ten**, cur**tain**, cer**tain**, heigh**ten**, tigh**ten**, fat**ten**, frigh**ten**, bea**ten** |

B27
🎧 Sentences
1. I cer**tain**ly need a nice white cot**ton** shirt with but**ton**s.
2. The police threa**ten**ed to tigh**ten** the rules for entering the country.
3. You must always be cer**tain** to tigh**ten** the cords when hanging your cur**tain**s.

B28
🎧 Verses

Listen and copy the intonation and voice modulation on the AUDIO TRACKS.

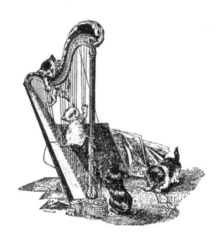

Three little kit**ten**s
They lost their mit**ten**s,
And they began to cry:
Oh, mother dear,
We sadly fear
Our mit**ten**s we have lost.
What! Lost your mit**ten**s,
You naughty kit**ten**s!
Then you shall have no pie.

B29

🎧 Articulation exercise: Major-General

I am the very model of a modern Major-General
I've information vegetable, animal and
mineral.
I know the kings of England and I quote the
fights historical
From Marathon to Waterloo, in order
categorical;
I'm very well acquainted too with matters
mathematical.
I understand equations, both the simple and
quadratical,
About binomial theorem I'm teeming with a
lot of news –
With many cheerful facts about the square of
the hypotenuse.
I'm very good at integral and differential calculus;
I know the scientific names of beings animalculous;
In short, in matters vegetable, animal and mineral,
I am the very model of a modern Major-General.
(*W.S. Gilbert*)

Additional exercises:

A: *Write down 4 words with the target sound that you often use when speaking English. Practice these words, thinking about your lips, tongue and jaw positions for the target sound.*

1. _____   3. _____

B: *Write down 4 words with the target sound that you often hear on TV, radio or from your friends/colleagues. Practice these words, thinking about your lips, tongue and jaw positions for the target sound.*

1. _____   3. _____

Lesson 29: Plosive consonants voiced [d] as in "dog"

B30

🎧 **Repeat once from left to right:**

d	d	d	d
dd	dd	dd	d
ddd	ddd	ddd	d
dddd	dddd	dddd	d

B31

🎧 **Words: voiced [d] sound**

> drought, durable, did, done, drill, drag, dwell, dangerous, debit, discount, damage, diminish, diversified, dedicate, direct

B32

🎧 **Comparison: [t] and [d]**

[t]	[d]
cart	card
tell	dwell
write	ride
tree	dream
trout	drought
tart	bard

B33

🎧 **Sentences: voiced [d] sound**

1. Due diligence revealed double standards in the production of different brands.
2. Douglas' daughter Deborah turned out to be a distinguished dancer.
3. I've studied the documentation for the new kidney drug in detail.
4. The dedicated student devoted to drama achieved dramatic results of immense depth.

72

B34

🎧 **Verses**

Tormente**d** with the anguished
drea**d**
Of falsehoo**d** unatone**d**,
I lay upon my sleepless be**d**,
And tossed and turne**d** an' groane**d**.

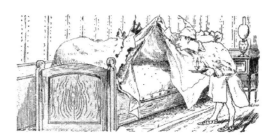

B35

🎧 **Articulation exercise**

What a to do to die today at a minute or two to two
A thing distinctly hard to say but harder still to do
For they'll beat a tattoo at twenty to two a Ra ta ta ta ta ta ta ta ta too
And the dragon will come when he hears the drum
At a minute or two to two today at a minute or two to two.

Held [d] followed by [n] sound

When [d] followed by [n], the tip of the tongue stays on the alveolar ridge, while the two sounds are made at the same time and the breath escapes through the nose.

B36

🎧 **Words**

dn₁ hid**den**, bur**den**, sad**den**, Hay**dn**, par**don**, sud**den**, mad**den**, mai**den**, glad**den**, har**den**, sud**den**ly, gar**den**

B37

🎧 **Sentences**

[dn₁]
1. A frightened mai**den** has been hid**den** in the rear gar**den**.
2. Hay**dn** is not a modern composer but his music will either sad**den**, glad**den** or mad**den** you.

Lesson 30: Plosive consonants unvoiced [k] as in "kind" and voiced [g] as in "gloss"

Speech organs position:

The tip of the tongue behind the bottom teeth, it's the back of the tongue going right up to make contact with the soft palate at the back of the roof of the mouth, and that forms the blockage. Then let the tongue come down and the air escapes in that little explosion and you get [k]; add voice and you get [g].

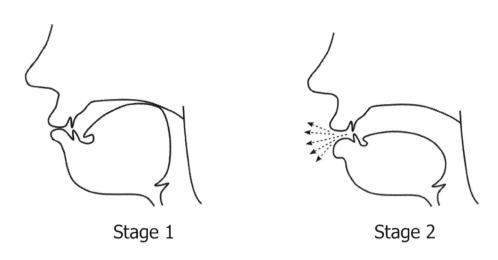

Stage 1   Stage 2

B38

🎧 **Repeat once from left to right:**

k	k	k	k
kk	kk	kk	k
kkk	kkk	kkk	k
kkkk	kkkk	kkkk	k

B39

🎧 **Words: the unvoiced [k] sound**

Spelling variations for the [k] sound	Highlighted bold letters pronounced as [k]
k	s**k**etch, **k**eep, **K**enya, **k**etchup, **k**ey, **k**ind
q	**q**uite, **q**uick, re**q**uest, s**q**ueeze, anti**q**ue
c	**c**at, **c**urious, magi**c**, un**c**le, histori**c**al, holisti**c**
ch	**ch**arismatic, stoma**ch**, **ch**emist, **ch**aos, **ch**ord

B40
🎧 Sentences: the unvoiced [k] sound

Listen and repeat. Read each sentence aloud slowly at first, then as if you were telling it to someone in a natural way.

1. **K**urt **c**an't **k**eep his **c**ool when **c**riticized by his un**c**le.
2. **C**atastrophi**c** reper**c**ussions **c**oncerning **ch**aotic **c**onfusion in **c**leri**c**al cir**c**les were **k**ept **q**uiet.
3. "**C**ut your **c**oat ac**c**ording to your **c**loth." *(Proverb)*
4. **Ch**arismati**c** **C**lara was **k**een to wear **k**in**k**y **c**lothes.
5. **C**onstance **c**olle**c**ted **c**oins and **c**ostumes from **C**anada and **C**ambodia.

B41
🎧 Verses

There was a **c**roo**k**ed man,
And he wal**k**ed a **c**roo**k**ed mile,
He found a **c**roo**k**ed sixpence
Against a **c**roo**k**ed stile;
He bought a **c**roo**k**ed **c**at,
Which **c**aught a **c**roo**k**ed mouse,
And they all lived together
In a little **c**roo**k**ed house.

Additional exercises:

A: *Write down 4 words with the target sound that you often use when speaking English. Practice these words, thinking about your lips, tongue and jaw positions for the target sound.*

1. _____ 3. _____

B: *Write down 4 words with the target sound that you often hear on TV, radio or from your friends/colleagues. Practice these words, thinking about your lips, tongue and jaw positions for the target sound.*

1. _____ 3. _____

B42

🎧 **Repeat once from left to right:**

g	g	g	g
gg	gg	gg	g
ggg	ggg	ggg	g
gggg	gggg	gggg	g

B43

🎧 **Words: voiced [g] sound**

Spelling variations for the [g] sound	Highlighted bold letters pronounced as [g]
g	**g**uessed, **g**uard, **g**host, pla**g**ue, **g**lue, stru**gg**le, an**g**le, sin**g**le, si**g**nal, lan**g**uage
x-[gz]	e**x**act, e**x**amination, e**x**aggerate, e**x**ert, e**x**asperate, e**x**isting

B44

🎧 **Comparison: [k] and [g]**

[k]	[g]
cream	**g**raze
re**q**uest	ru**g**by
climax	**g**lass
coast	**gh**ost
con	**g**one

B45

🎧 **Sentences: voiced [g] sound**

Listen and repeat. Read each sentence aloud slowly at first, then as if you were telling it to someone in a natural way.

1. **G**ladys **g**lanced at **G**raham and **g**ave him a va**g**ue **gigg**le.
2. **G**race stru**gg**led with her **G**reek **g**rammar e**x**am and was **g**lad to **g**et a **g**reat **g**rade.
3. **G**ilbert **G**reen is no lon**g**er a single **g**uy.
4. **G**racious **G**loria **g**azed at the e**x**aggerated **g**leaming **g**lobe.
5. "**G**ood **g**racious," the **g**rey **gh**ost said, "the fo**g** is **g**etting thicker."

B46
🎧 Tongue-twister

Three **g**rey **g**eese in a **g**reen field **g**razing,
Green were the **g**eese and **g**reen was the
grazing.

B47
🎧 Articulation exercise

pt	pt	pt	pt
kt	kt	kt	kt
ptkt	ptkt	ptkt	ptkt
bd	bd	bd	bd
gd	gd	gd	gd
bdgd	bdgd	bdgd	bdgd

Lesson 31: Nasal consonant [m] as in "monk"

Description of nasal consonants:

Two blockages to make the breath go straight into the nose. First of all the most important blockage is at the soft palate which is right at the back of the roof of the mouth; it actually is lowered, so that it stops the breath from coming from the lungs and the throat into the mouth and it has to come up and out of the nose. At the same time we have three little positions of the speech organs which also form the blockage in the case of: [m], [n] and [ŋ].

Speech organs position:

[m]: the lips come together, so that the breath cannot escape; the sound is produced in the nose.

B48

🎧 **Words: the [m] sound**

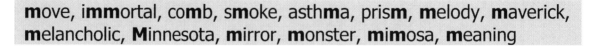

move, immortal, comb, smoke, asthma, prism, melody, maverick, melancholic, Minnesota, mirror, monster, mimosa, meaning

B49

🎧 **Sentences: the [m] sound**

1. The **m**anager fro**m M**ichigan reco**mm**ended **m**aking **m**ore **m**oney.
2. **M**ozart's **m**elancholic **m**elodies have botto**m**less **m**eaning.
3. "The **m**oon looks like a **m**ottled **m**elon," **m**ur**m**ured **M**ark.
4. **M**argaret **m**ust be on ti**m**e for her **m**orning lessons in **m**i**m**e.
5. **M**aps **m**ade in **M**alaysia **m**eet the needs of the **m**ost de**m**anding of custo**m**ers.

78

B50
🎧 Tongue-twister: the [m] sound

Hie to the **m**arket, **Mim**i come trot,
Spilt all her butter **m**ilk, every drop.
Every drop and every dra**m**,
Mimi ca**m**e ho**m**e with an e**m**pty can.

B51
🎧 Articulation exercise

My boy you may take it from me,
That of all the afflictions accursed
With which a man's saddled and hampered and addled,
A diffident nature's the worst.
Though clever as clever can be
A Crichton of early romance
You must stir it and stump it and blow your own trumpet,
Or trust me you haven't a chance!

Now take for example my case
I've a bright intellectual brain
In all London city there's no one so witty –
I thought so again and again.
I've a highly intelligent face –
My features cannot be denied –
But whatever I try, Sir, I fail in, and why Sir?
I'm modesty personified!

Additional exercises:

A: *Write down 4 words with the target sound that you often use when speaking English. Practice these words, thinking about your lips, tongue and jaw positions for the target sound.*

1. _____ 3. _____

B: *Write down 4 words with the target sound that you often hear on TV, radio or from your friends/colleagues. Practice these words, thinking about your lips, tongue and jaw positions for the target sound.*

1. _____ 3. _____

Lesson 32: Nasal consonant [n] as in "nun"

Speech organs position:
The tip of the tongue is
on the alveolar ridge, but the
soft palate coming down, the
sound is produced in the nose.
Keep the tongue still while making
the sound and then relax.

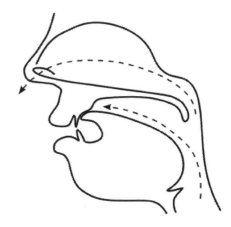

B52
🎧 Words

Spelling variations for the [n] sound	Highlighted bold letters pronounced as [n]
n	**n**oble, **n**u**nn**ery, **n**imble, **n**aughty, **n**i**n**e, **n**ever, **n**est, law**n**, daw**n**, upo**n**, dow**n**, pe**n**ny, agai**n**, so**n**
kn	**kn**it, **kn**owledge, **kn**own, **Kn**icks

B53
🎧 Sentences

1. **N**i**n**a would**n**'t give her pho**n**e **n**umber to just a**n**yo**n**e.
2. I **n**either u**n**dersta**n**d **n**or i**n**sta**n**tly admire ig**n**ora**n**t, **n**arrow-mi**n**ded, opi**n**io**n**ated me**n** without i**nn**er fire.
3. A**nn**e fi**n**ds the **n**ews from foreig**n** la**n**ds i**n**formative a**n**d i**n**teresting.
4. **N**aughty **N**ick s**n**eaked off to Au**n**t A**nn**ie's bar**n** a**n**d **n**apped till **n**oon like a buffoo**n**.
5. At **n**i**n**e i**n** the mor**n**ing, the trai**n** for **N**ew York comes dow**n** the li**n**e.
6. **N**either **N**i**n**a **n**or **N**ita **n**eeded **n**ew **kn**itted **n**ighties.

B54

🎧 Verses

For every evil u**n**der the su**n**,
There is a remedy or there is **n**o**n**e.
If there be o**n**e, try a**n**d fi**n**d it;
If there be **n**o**n**e, **n**ever mi**n**d it.

Additional exercises:

A: *Write down 4 words with the target sound that you often use when speaking English. Practice these words, thinking about your lips, tongue and jaw positions for the target sound.*

1. _____   3. _____

2. _____   4. _____

B: *Write down 4 words with the target sound that you often hear on TV, radio or from your friends/colleagues. Practice these words, thinking about your lips, tongue and jaw positions for the target sound.*

1. _____   3. _____

2. _____   4. _____

Lesson 33: Nasal consonant [ŋ] as in "king"

Speech organs position:
The tip of the tongue is down behind the bottom teeth, but the back of the tongue goes up to the soft palate, forming a blockage.

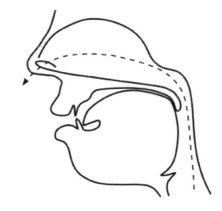

B55

🎧 **Words: the [ŋ] sound**

Spelling variations for [ŋ]	Highlighted bold letters pronounced as [ŋ]
ng	wi**ng**, si**ng**, su**ng**, ri**ng**, ha**ng**, bri**ng**, cli**ng**, sti**ng**, amo**ng**, to**ng**ue, nothi**ng**, saili**ng**, raili**ng**
n before k	thi**n**k, wi**n**k, ba**n**k, ho**n**k

B56

🎧 **Sentences: the [ŋ] sound**

1. The you**ng** si**ng**er was si**ng**i**ng** a rousi**ng** so**ng**.
2. At the beginni**ng** of this morni**ng**'s class we were practici**ng** to**ng**ue exercises.
3. Without thi**n**ki**ng**, the Ki**ng** swu**ng** on the bell and it ra**ng** with a ti**ng**-a-li**ng**.
4. Payi**ng** rent, commuti**ng**, eati**ng** and dri**n**ki**ng** has been taki**ng** all the money I was earni**ng** from typi**ng**, writi**ng**, and publicisi**ng**.
5. Supposi**ng** he is comi**ng** for a meeti**ng**, will you be telli**ng** him about separati**ng** and leavi**ng** Lansi**ng**?

B57

🎧 **Verses: the [ŋ] sound**

Don't display a lot of stocki**ng**,
Which is always very shocki**ng**,
But of course I'm only mocki**ng**!

Additional exercises:

A: *Write down 4 words with the target sound that you often use when speaking English. Practice these words, thinking about your lips, tongue and jaw positions for the target sound.*

1. _____ 3. _____

2. _____ 4. _____

B: *Write down 4 words with the target sound that you often hear on TV, radio or from your friends/colleagues. Practice these words, thinking about your lips, tongue and jaw positions for the target sound.*

1. _____ 3. _____

2. _____ 4. _____

Lesson 34: Lateral consonant [l] as in "link"

Speech organs position:
Air escapes out of the side of the tongue. The tip of the tongue is on the alveolar ridge and the back of the tongue down; the breath has to come out of the side of the tongue to escape.

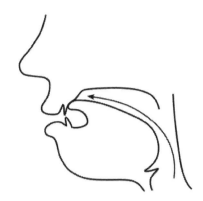

B58
🎧 Words

> leave, last, letter, love, lend, alone, allow, silly, chilly, fellow, shallow, holy, hollow, believe, place, plastic, blame, blue, blood, glue, glow, click, cloth, clumsy, club

B59
🎧 Sentences

1. "When life hands you a lemon, make lemonade." *(Harry Truman)*
2. Luminous lamps light the whole hall beautifully.
3. Luke's ludicrous letters to Lucy are unbelievable.
4. She looked supple and elegant in her black Chanel jacket.
5. Red leather, yellow leather, red leather, yellow leather.
6. Failure to calculate the yield of the field made the clever lad ill.

B60

🎧 **Verses**

Luke Lock likes lakes.
Luke's dog likes lakes.
Luke Lock swims in lakes.
Luke's dog looks at lakes.
The dog takes a swim in lakes Luke Lock likes.
Luke Lock takes his dog in lakes dogs like.

Additional exercises:

A: *Write down 4 words with the target sound that you often use when speaking English. Practice these words, thinking about your lips, tongue and jaw positions for the target sound.*

1. _____ 3. _____

2. _____ 4. _____

B: *Write down 4 words with the target sound that you often hear on TV, radio or from your friends/colleagues. Practice these words, thinking about your lips, tongue and jaw positions for the target sound.*

1. _____ 3. _____

2. _____ 4. _____

Lesson 35: Fricative consonants unvoiced [f] as in "fun" and voiced [v] as in "value"

Description of the fricative consonants:

The passage of the air is not blocked completely; it is narrowed by two speech organs coming very close together, so the breath has to squeeze its way past and as it squeezes through the small gap sets a little bit of friction, and that friction creates a sound.

Speech organs position:

It's the top teeth which gently make contact with the bottom lip. The air can squeeze past. Without any sound it forms [f] as in "fish"; add sound to that, and you get [v].

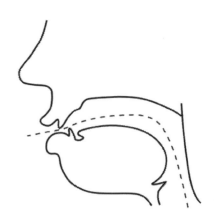

B61
🎧 Words: the unvoiced [f] sound

Spelling variations for the [f] sound	Highlighted bold letters pronounced as [f]
f	**f**east, **f**irst, cle**f**t, li**f**t, **f**antasy, **f**antastic, **f**inish
ft	so**ft**en, o**ft**en
ph	**ph**armacy, **ph**one, photogra**ph**, **ph**iloso**ph**y, **ph**ysics, **ph**ilharmonic
gh	rou**gh**, tou**gh**, lau**gh**

B62
🎧 Sentences: the unvoiced [f] sound

1. "**F**ine **f**eathers make **f**ine birds." *(Proverb)*
2. **Ph**ilip made an e**ff**ort to **f**ind his girl**f**riend's **f**avorite **f**uchsia **f**lowers.
3. An old **f**isherman lau**gh**ed when he caught **f**ive **f**resh **f**ish.
4. The **f**ifty friends **f**rom **f**ar-**f**lung **f**oreign lands **f**ormed a **f**raternity.

B63

🎧 **Verses: the unvoiced [f] sound**

Freddy **f**armer went to **F**resno
And went **f**ishing in the **f**og.
When he thought he'd caught a **f**ish
In **f**act he caught a **f**rog!

B64

🎧 **Words: the voiced [v] sound**

vote, **v**irtue, de**v**elop, re**v**i**v**e, **viv**acious, in**v**ol**v**e, arri**v**e, con**v**ince, thri**v**e, sho**v**e, **v**acuum, Ste**v**en, re**v**i**v**al, **v**inegar, **v**olume, **v**elour

B65

🎧 **Comparison: [f] and [v]**

[f]	[v]
fat	**v**at
file	**v**ile
fail	**v**ale
shi**f**t	sho**v**e
e**ff**ort	e**v**idence
focus	**v**ocal

B66

🎧 Sentences: the voiced [v] sound

1. Effer**v**escent **V**era tried to achie**v**e mar**v**ellous results in **v**ain.
2. **V**indicti**v**e **v**endors con**v**inced nai**v**e **V**ictor to buy o**v**erpriced **v**el**v**et and **v**elour.

3. **Viv**acious **Viv**ian loved to **v**oice **v**igorous **v**erses **v**ociferously.
4. Ste**v**en **v**ainly **v**iewed **v**ast **v**ales with **v**acant eyes.
5. "There are **v**ery many **v**arieties of **v**egetation on our **v**eranda," said **V**era.

B67

🎧 Verses: the [v] sound

Vera **v**aulted **v**ainly o**v**er the garden wall,
Vera **v**ery nearly had a nasty fall.

Additional exercises:

A: *Write down 4 words with the target sound that you often use when speaking English. Practice these words, thinking about your lips, tongue and jaw positions for the target sound.*

1. _____   3. _____

2. _____   4. _____

B: *Write down 4 words with the target sound that you often hear on TV, radio or from your friends/colleagues. Practice these words, thinking about your lips, tongue and jaw positions for the target sound.*

1. _____   3. _____

2. _____   4. _____

Lesson 36: Unvoiced consonant [θ] as in "think"

Speech organs position:

The tip of the tongue comes between top and bottom teeth gently, breath squeezes past, we hear the unvoiced [θ], as in "think"; add sound to the same process and you get [ð], as in "the".

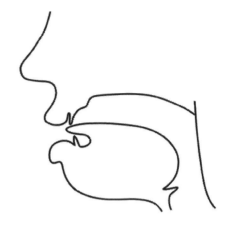

B68

🎧 **Words**

th	**th**anks, **th**ree, **th**ird, **th**ought, **th**umb, **th**ing, **th**in, ba**th**, brea**th**, clo**th**, ten**th**, six**th**, tru**th**, bo**th**, au**th**or, ari**th**metic

B69

🎧 **Sentences**

1. **Th**ree fil**th**y-looking **th**ieves were hiding in the **th**icket of **th**orny **th**istle bushes.
2. The au**th**or revealed the uncou**th** tru**th** in his latest **th**riller.
3. **Th**elma **th**ought that **th**eocratic **th**inking was **th**rilling.
4. **Th**eoretical ma**th** comes from **th**orough **th**inking of en**th**usiastic ari**th**meticians.
5. One weal**th**y au**th**or only wrote the tru**th** and not fil**th**.

B70
🎧 Comparison: [t] and [θ]

[t]	[θ]
taught	thought
trick	thick
tin	thin
note	north
matt	mouth
trade	thread
met	math

B71
🎧 Verses

A **Th**atcher of **Th**atchwood went to **Th**atcher a-**th**atching;
Did the of **Th**atcher of **Th**atchwood go to **Th**atcher a-**th**atching ?
If a **Th**atcher of **Th**atchwood went to **Th**atcher a-**th**atching,
Where is the **th**atching **th**e **th**atcher of **Th**atchwood has **th**atched?

Additional exercises:

A: *Write down 4 words with the target sound that you often use when speaking English. Practice these words, thinking about your lips, tongue and jaw positions for the target sound.*

1. _____ 3. _____

B: *Write down 4 words with the target sound that you often hear on TV, radio or from your friends/colleagues. Practice these words, thinking about your lips, tongue and jaw positions for the target sound.*

1. _____ 3. _____

Lesson 37: Voiced consonant [ð] as in "mother"

Speech organs position:
The tip of the tongue comes between the top lip and bottom lip and the air squeezes past. Add voice for [ð] sound.

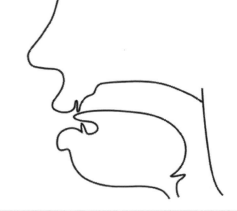

B72
🎧 **Words**

> though, **that**, **th**erefore, **than**, ba**the**, smoo**th**, clo**the**, soo**the**, brea**the**, fa**the**r, o**the**r, ga**the**r, ra**the**r, fur**the**r, ei**the**r

B73
🎧 **Sentences**

1. **Th**is medicine is soo**th**ing for my ra**the**r sore back.
2. I would ra**the**r buy **th**is lea**the**r hat **than** **th**at one wi**th the** fea**th**ers.
3. My mo**the**r and fa**the**r adore my younger bro**the**r for being smarter **than** I.
4. **Th**is brown lea**the**r coat is made of smoo**the**r lea**the**r **than** **th**at black one in **the** window.
5. **The** sou**the**rly wind blew **th**is way and **th**at across **the** pinky hea**the**r.
6. Birds of a fea**the**r flock toge**the**r.
7. **The** pen is mightier **than the** sword.

B74
🎧 **Verses**

From **th**is to **th**at she hops about
Then back to **th**is as if in doubt.

92

Additional exercises:

A: *Write down 4 words with the target sound that you often use when speaking English. Practice these words, thinking about your lips, tongue and jaw positions for the target sound.*

1. _____   3. _____

2. _____   4. _____

B: *Write down 4 words with the target sound that you often hear on TV, radio or from your friends/colleagues. Practice these words, thinking about your lips, tongue and jaw positions for the target sound.*

1. _____   3. _____

2. _____   4. _____

Lesson 38: Unvoiced [s] as in "son" and voiced [z] as in "zigzag"

Speech organs position:
The air escapes through a narrow passage along the centre of the tongue which squeezes between the top of the tongue and the alveolar ridge and you get [s] as in "sip"; add sound and you get [z].

B75
🎧 **Words**: the unvoiced [s] sound

Spelling variations for the [s] sound	Highlighted bold letters pronounced as [s]
s	**s**wan, ba**s**e, cha**s**e, paradi**s**e, promi**s**e, ga**s**, atla**s**, take**s**
sc	**sc**ientific, **sc**ience, **sc**ent
c	finan**c**e, **c**emetery, **c**ircumstan**c**es, re**c**eive, practi**c**e

B76
🎧 **Sentences: the unvoiced [s] sound**

1. **S**ort these book**s** on the **s**taircase a**s** **s**oon as you have a **s**pare **s**econd.
2. For **s**upper, we've been **s**erved ta**s**ty **s**word fish with lemon **s**au**c**e and **s**ucculent **s**alad.
3. The **s**ymphony **s**eemed **s**ad and **s**entimental.
4. **S**imon **s**aw **s**even **s**ilver **s**wift**s** in the **s**ea.
5. **S**teven **S**mith **s**tood **s**even foot **s**ix in his **s**tocking feet.

B77
🎧 Verses: the unvoiced [s] sound

Steven thought he **s**ang **s**o **s**weetly
In his offi**c**e every day,
But **s**o tunele**ss** was his **s**inging
He was paid to go away...

It'**s** a grea**s**y kind of pa**s**try,
Which, perhap**s**, a judgement ha**s**ty
Some might find
rather ta**s**ty.

B78
🎧 Words: the voiced [z] sound

Spelling variations for the [z] sound	Highlighted bold letters pronounced as [z]
z	**z**oom, **z**ealous, **z**ip, **z**igzag, **z**oo, **Z**urich, **z**inc, **z**ebra, **z**ero, **z**est, **Z**imbabwe
s	sci**ss**or**s**, u**s**e, doe**s**, ha**s**, i**s**, a**s**, wa**s**, ea**s**y, bu**s**y, dog**s**, tree**s**, play**s**, clean**s**e

Voiced and unvoiced endings for plurals and third person singulars

Rule: If the sound before the ending is unvoiced then the ending will be unvoiced too. If the sound before the ending is voiced then the ending will be voiced.

Unvoiced sounds (sounds made with breath only)	**Voiced sounds** (sounds made with vibrations of vocal cords)
1) Consonant Pairs: [s] soup [p] pick [t] tick [k] kick	**1) Consonant Pairs:** [z] hose [b] bubble [d] dog [g] giggle

95

[tʃ] church [ʃ] shoe [f] fan [θ] think	[dʒ] George [ʒ] rouge [v] van [ð] that **2) Voiced nasal and lateral consonants:** [l] lock, [m] meter, [n] nun, [ŋ] king **3) All vowels and diphthongs**

B79
🎧 **Comparison: [s] and [z]**

[s]	[z]
docks	dogs
hats	homes
hits	hums
cakes	kegs
nits	nuns
bits	bids
kicks	fans
cats	cads
pets	feds
mats	moms
shocks	gigs
cooks	girls
mistakes	problems

B80
🎧 Sentences: the voiced [z] sound

1. Always keep your eyes on the prize!
2. Joseph supposes that his toeses are roses.
3. **Z**eta rode a **z**ebra in **Z**imbabwe.
4. Ideas do not fall from the trees.
5. **Z**oë spends dollars and dollars on snazzy shoes and gowns.
6. The bee buzzes lazily on the pansies, daisies and roses.
7. "Beggars can't be choosers." *(Proverb)*

B81
🎧 Verses: the voiced [z] sound

Scissors and string, scissors and string,
When a man's single he lives like a king.
Needles and pins, needles and pins,
When a man marries his trouble begins.

Additional exercises:

A: *Write down 4 words with the target sound that you often use when speaking English. Practice these words, thinking about your lips, tongue and jaw positions for the target sound.*

1. _____   3. _____

2. _____   4. _____

B: *Write down 4 words with the target sound that you often hear on TV, radio or from your friends/colleagues. Practice these words, thinking about your lips, tongue and jaw positions for the target sound.*

1. _____   3. _____

2. _____   4. _____

Lesson 39: Unvoiced [ʃ] as in "shock" and voiced [ʒ] as in "vision"

Speech organs position:

The tongue tip near the bottom of the mouth. It is the front of the tongue that comes up to almost the alveolar ridge and the little bit of hard palate next to it. As the breath squeezes past, we get [ʃ], as in "shall"; add sound and we get [ʒ], as in "measure". The tongue tip does not come to the alveolar ridge for that.

B82

🎧 Words: the unvoiced [ʃ] sound

Spelling variations for the [ʃ] sound	Highlighted bold letters pronounced as [ʃ]
sh	**sh**eep, **sh**irt, pu**sh**, wi**sh**, fa**sh**ion, ca**sh**ier
ch	mousta**ch**e, **ch**ampagne
s, ss	pre**ss**ure, se**ss**ion, Ru**ss**ia, **s**ure, **S**ean
Spelling variations for the [ʃə] sound	Highlighted bold letters pronounced as [ʃə]
cio, cia	spe**cia**l, deli**cio**us, mali**cio**us, suspi**cio**us
tio, cia	condi**tio**n, mo**tio**n, nutri**tio**us, Vene**tia**n

B83

🎧 Sentences: the unvoiced [ʃ] sound

1. I wi**sh** I **sh**opped for **sh**irts with fa**sh**ionable **Sh**eila.
2. During our spe**cia**l se**ssi**on on nutri**tio**n we wi**sh**ed to be served deli**cio**us di**sh**es and **ch**ampagne.
3. **S**ean's **sh**iny **sh**oes are made from **sh**ark skin.
4. Mali**cio**us men with mousta**ch**es pre**ss**ured us to leave the **sh**ip.
5. **Sh**immering and **sh**ining hair needs a **sh**ampoo and a condi**tio**ner.
6. "**Sh**are and **sh**are alike." *(Proverb)*

98

B84

🎧 **Tongue-twister: the unvoiced [ʃ] sound**

She sells sea**sh**ells by the sea-**sh**ore;
If **sh**e sells sea**sh**ells by the sea-**sh**ore,
Then I'm **s**ure **sh**e sells sea-**sh**ore **sh**ells.

B85

🎧 **Words: the voiced [ʒ] sound**

Spelling variations for the [ʒ] sound	Highlighted bold letters pronounced as [ʒ]
s before **u, ur**	mea**su**re, plea**su**re, ca**su**al, enclo**su**re
s before **io**	occa**sio**n, deci**sio**n, confu**sio**n, intru**sio**n, colli**sio**n
g	presti**g**e, gara**g**e, massa**g**e, bei**g**e, rou**g**e

B86

🎧 **Comparison: [ʃ] and [ʒ]**

[ʃ]	[ʒ]
condi**tio**n	colli**si**on
shoes	unu**su**al
a**ss**ure	ca**su**al
vi**cio**us	vi**si**on
vaca**tio**ns	occa**si**on
devo**tio**n	deci**si**on

B87

🎧 **Sentences: the voiced [ʒ] sound**

Listen and repeat. Read each sentence aloud slowly at first, then as if you were telling it to someone in a natural way.

1. Charles trea**su**red the presti**g**e of his house and disliked sudden intru**sio**n.
2. Disillu**sio**ned **J**acque felt confu**sio**n regarding the disclo**su**re of the family trea**su**re.
3. Watching televi**sio**n without mea**su**re can be a limiting plea**su**re.

4. The girl u**su**ally uses red rou**g**e but she decided to change to bei**g**e.

5. **G**iselle strives for preci**si**on in her dress**ag**e supervi**si**on.

B88
🎧 **Articulation exercise**

Oh a private buffoon is a light hearted
loon,
If you listen to popular rumor.
From the morn to the night he's so joyous and bright
And he bubbles with wit and good humor.
He's so quaint and so terse, both in prose and in verse,
Yet though people forgive his transgressions,
There are one or two rules that all Family Fools
Must observe if they love their profession.
There are one or two rules, half a dozen maybe
That all Family Fools of whatever degree,
Must observe, if they love their profession.

B89
🎧 **Verses: the voiced [ʒ] sound**
Oh, marvellous illu**si**on!
Or, terrible surprise!
What is this strange confu**si**on
That veils my aching eyes?

Additional exercises:

A: *Write down 4 words with the target sound that you often use when speaking English. Practice these words, thinking about your lips, tongue and jaw positions for the target sound.*

1. _____   3. _____

2. _____   4. _____

B: *Write down 4 words with the target sound that you often hear on TV, radio or from your friends/colleagues. Practice these words, thinking about your lips, tongue and jaw positions for the target sound.*

1. _____   3. _____

2. _____   4. _____

Lesson 40: Unvoiced consonant [h] as in "hat"

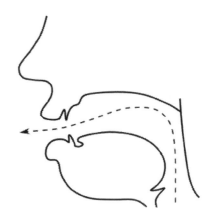

Speech organs position:
The passage of breath is narrowed by moving the vocal chords from wide apart to close together. Friction is heard when the breath squeezes between them.

B90
🎧 **Words**

h	**h**at, **h**eat, **h**ard, **h**urt, **h**ideous, a**h**oy, be**h**ind, be**h**ave, per**h**aps, boy**h**ood, re**h**earse, en**h**ance, **h**eather, **h**eredity, in**h**erit, ad**h**ere, dis**h**earten, be**h**alf
wh	**wh**o

B91
🎧 **Sentences**

1. On be**h**alf of the **wh**ole group, we say a **h**earty **h**ello.
2. Be**h**ind **h**is **h**ideous be**h**avior, which was **h**urting us to the very **h**eart, was **h**is **h**ard child**h**ood.
3. In case of a **h**orrible **h**eadache, **h**eat **wh**olesome **h**eather **h**oney and in**h**ale it.
4. **H**eather in**h**erited **h**er father's **h**orrendously **h**uge **h**ouse in the **H**amptons.
5. **H**ungarian **h**unters on **h**orses with **h**ounds were **h**orrified by **h**urricanes.
6. "**Wh**o," said **H**elen, "**h**as eaten **h**alf of my **h**oney cake?"

B92
🎧 **Verses**

Henry Harvey heaved a huge and heavy hammer,
A huge and heavy hammer Henry Harvey heaved,
If Henry Harvey heaved a huge and heavy
hammer,
Where's the huge and heavy hammer Henry
Harvey heaved?

Additional exercises:

A: *Write down 4 words with the target sound that you often use when speaking English. Practice these words, thinking about your lips, tongue and jaw positions for the target sound.*

1. _____   3. _____

2. _____   4. _____

B: *Write down 4 words with the target sound that you often hear on TV, radio or from your friends/colleagues. Practice these words, thinking about your lips, tongue and jaw positions for the target sound.*

1. _____   3. _____

2. _____   4. _____

Lesson 41: The [r] sound as in "rat"

Speech organs position:
Tip of the tongue curling back in the roof of the mouth, just behind the alveolar ridge, and the breath literally squeezes past.

[r   r   r]

B93
🎧 *Repeat once from left to right:*

[ru	roʊ	rɔ	rɑ	reɪ	ri]
[pr u	proʊ	prɔ	prɑ	preɪ	pri]
[spr u	sproʊ	sprɔ	sprɑ	spreɪ	spri]
[gr u	groʊ	grɔ	grɑ	greɪ	gri]
[br u	broʊ	brɔ	brɑ	breɪ	bri]
[fr u	froʊ	frɔ	frɑ	freɪ	fri]
[θr u	θroʊ	θrɔ	θrɑ	θreɪ	θri]

B94
🎧 **Words**

r	rang, rest, road, rock, rascal, rescue
pr	proof, proud, press, prank, pressure
spr	spread, sprawl, sprain, spring, sprout
cr	crime, crawl, cruise, cry, crept, cross
gr	grand, grain, grass, gravy, grows
br	bring, brave, break, brute, browse
fr	fry, frame, fright, frank, frost, freeze
thr	thrift, threat, throb, through, thrill
rr	borrow, sorrow, carry, worry, carriage

B95
🎧 Sentences

1. **R**iding around the na**rr**ow **r**ace-t**r**ack,
   Robert **r**an over a ho**rr**id b**r**own **r**at.
2. **R**ound and **r**ound the **r**ugged **r**ock, the
   ragged **r**ascal **r**an.
3. In spring, **R**ome is **r**eally very p**r**etty.
4. **R**ose **R**ochester's **r**ole emb**r**aces
   p**r**eparation of the p**r**ofiles for **r**egional sales **r**eps.
5. I p**r**efer p**r**awns on **r**ye b**r**ead to g**r**easy po**r**k with g**r**avy and **r**ice.

B96
🎧 Tongue-twister

Robert **R**owley **r**olled a **r**ound **r**oll a**r**ound,
A **r**ound **r**oll **R**obert **R**owley **r**olled a**r**ound;
Where **r**olled the **r**ound **r**oll
Robert **R**owley **r**olled a**r**ound?

Additional exercises:

A: *Write down 4 words with the target sound that you often use when speaking English. Practice these words, thinking about your lips, tongue and jaw positions for the target sound.*

1. _____ 3. _____

2. _____ 4. _____

B: *Write down 4 words with the target sound that you often hear on TV, radio or from your friends/colleagues. Practice these words, thinking about your lips, tongue and jaw positions for the target sound.*

1. _____ 3. _____

2. _____ 4. _____

Lesson 42: Affricates unvoiced [tʃ] as in "church" and voiced [dʒ] as in "gin"

Affricates are simply double consonants and they consist of one plosive consonant followed by one fricative consonant. They both have to match, they are either both unvoiced or both voiced.

Speech organs position:

[tʃ], as in "church": plosive [t] as in "time", made at exactly the same time as fricative consonant [ʃ] as in "shall". They have the position of both. Add sound and you get [d] allied with [ʒ] and you end up with the voiced [dʒ].

B97
🎧 Words: the [tʃ] sound

Spelling variations for the [tʃ] sound	Highlighted bold letters pronounced as [tʃ]
ch	**ch**ur**ch**, **ch**ap, whi**ch**, or**ch**ard, a**ch**ieve
tch	ca**tch**, bu**tch**er, clu**tch**ed, ma**tch**ed, wa**tch**
t before u	litera**tu**re, pos**tu**re, mois**tu**rize, architec**tu**re

B98
🎧 Sentences: the unvoiced [tʃ] sound

1. The old **ch**ur**ch** in **Ch**elsea represents the architec**tu**re of the eighteenth cen**tu**ry.
2. The lec**tu**re in **Ch**inese litera**tu**re was quite an adven**tu**re for the lec**tu**rer.
3. For lun**ch**, I had some na**ch**os with blue **ch**eese followed by **Ch**inese jasmine tea.
4. We **ch**eerfully **ch**ose mat**ch**ing **ch**airs to go with our **ch**arming furni**tu**re.
5. They **ch**ased and sear**ch**ed for **Ch**arlie but they couldn't cat**ch** **h**im.
6. If I ca**tch** her, I will pin**ch** her and scra**tch** her!

B99
🎧 Tongue-twister: the unvoiced [tʃ] sound

Listen and copy the intonation and voice modulation on the AUDIO TRACKS.

How mu**ch** wood would a wood**ch**uck **ch**uck
If a wood**ch**uck could **ch**uck wood?

B100
🎧 Words: the [dʒ] sound

Spelling variations for the [dʒ] sound	Highlighted bold letters pronounced as [dʒ]
j	**j**ob, ad**j**oin, **j**oke, **J**ohn, **J**une, **j**uvenile, re**j**ection
g	**g**em, lugga**g**e, ba**dg**er, le**dg**er, **G**eorge, coura**g**e

B101
🎧 Comparison: [tʃ] and [dʒ]

[tʃ]	[dʒ]
church	**J**u**dg**e
chap	**J**apan
cheap	**g**yp
chin	**g**in
chunk	**j**unk
choose	**j**uice
ba**tch**	bagga**g**e
adven**tu**re	avera**g**e

B102
🎧 Sentences: the voiced [dʒ] sound

1. In **J**une and **J**uly the weather is **g**enerally en**j**oyable in this re**g**ion of **G**eor**g**ia.
2. **J**ohn was **j**u**dg**ing his wife for re**j**ections in his marria**g**e and his boss for in**j**ustice in his **j**ob.
3. These gherkins with **g**in**g**er and tomato **j**uice from the **j**ar are **j**ust great!
4. Even an avera**g**e **j**u**dg**e char**g**es too much!
5. The marria**g**e of **G**erald and **G**ina was **j**u**dg**ed to be **j**oyful.

107

B103
🎧 **Verses: the voiced [dʒ] sound**

Yes, now I'm a Ju**dg**e!
Though all my law be fu**dg**e,
Yet I'll never, never bu**dg**e,
But I'll live and die a Ju**dg**e!
And a good Ju**dg**e too!

Additional exercises:

A: *Write down 4 words with the target sound that you often use when speaking English. Practice these words, thinking about your lips, tongue and jaw positions for the target sound.*

1. _____   3. _____

2. _____   4. _____

B: *Write down 4 words with the target sound that you often hear on TV, radio or from your friends/colleagues. Practice these words, thinking about your lips, tongue and jaw positions for the target sound.*

1. _____   3. _____

2. _____   4. _____

Lesson 43: Contractions

In good fluent speech the particle "not", verbs "to be" ("am, is, are"), "to have" ("has, had"), "will" and "would" are shortened. The shortened version of a word is called a contraction.

It's important to use contractions if you would like to sound fluent, natural and more like a native speaker of English.

Contractions are not usually used in written English except in dialogues and in informal writing.

C1
🎧 **Contractions of modal verbs**

Listen carefully and repeat the sentences, noting the pronunciation of the contracted verb "have".

Full form	Contraction	Pronunciation
could have	could've	[ˈkʊdəv]
might have	might've	[ˈmaɪtəv]
should have	should've	[ˈʃʊdəv]
must have	must've	[ˈmʌstəv]

Full form	Contraction
Could you have done it?	I could**'ve** done it if I knew how.
Might you have read it?	I might**'ve** read it if I was interested.
Have they arrived yet?	They should**'ve** done so by now.
Have you discussed it with any one?	I must**'ve** discussed it in the club.

C2
🎧 Contractions of the verb "has"

Listen carefully and repeat the sentences, noting the pronunciation of the contracted verb "has"

Full form "has" becomes a contraction, "s"

Full form "has "	Contraction "s"
He has moved away.	He**'s** moved away in order to be close to his office.
She has always worked hard.	She**'s** always worked hard to become successful.
It has been a difficult time.	It**'s** been a difficult time but the future's looking bright.
He has been doing it.	He**'s** been doing it for a long time.

C3
🎧 Contractions of the verb "had"

Listen carefully and repeat the sentences, noting the pronunciation of the contracted verb "had".

Full form "had "	Contraction "d"
I had always wanted it.	I**'d** always wanted to become an accountant.
You had already told me.	You**'d** already told me that the meeting was next week.
She had promised to deliver the contract.	She**'d** promised to deliver the contract; but, as it happened, she didn't.
I had sent my tax return.	I**'d** sent my tax return before I checked all the figures.

C4
🎧 Verb "to be"

Full form	Contractions	Pronunciation
I am	I'm	[aɪm]
it is	it's	[ɪts]
what is	what's	[wɒts]
we are	we're	[wiːə]
they are	they're	[ðeɪə]

C5
🎧 Full form, "I am", becomes a contraction, "I'm"

Listen carefully and repeat the sentences, noting the pronunciation of the contracted verb.

1. I'm done here; I'm finally leaving.
2. I'm sorry I'm such a mess.
3. I'm feeling very uncomfortable about it.
4. I'm on the horns of a dilemma.

Full form of the verb "is" becomes a contraction, "s"

1. What's wrong with you?
2. For what it's worth, I am very sorry.
3. That's the least of our worries.
4. It's possible she might've misunderstood us.

Full form of the verb "are" becomes a "contraction, "re" [ə]

1. They're going away.
2. You're right about that.
3. We're about to leave.

C6
🎧 **Contractions of the verb "will" becomes a contraction "ll"**

Listen carefully and repeat the sentences, noting the pronunciation of the contracted verb.

1. You**'ll** need to find a better way to deal with your boss.
2. I**'ll** sum it up for you.
3. I**'ll** keep my mouth shut, not that it**'ll** keep me from losing my job.

You**'ll** never guess what**'s** just happened.

C7
🎧 **The verb "would" becomes a contraction "d"**

Listen carefully and repeat the sentences, noting the pronunciation of the contracted verb.

1. I**'d** like to weigh in here.
2. We**'d** like to end this meeting now.
3. If you**'d** excuse me, I**'d** rather not discuss it.
4. I**'d** like to point out that I**'m** running late.

C8
🎧 **Contraction of negative verbs**

Listen carefully and repeat the sentences, noting the pronunciation of the contracted verb.

Written form	Contractions	Pronunciation
do not	don't	[dəʊnt]
does not	doesn't	[dʌznt]
is not	isn't	[ɪznt]
would not	wouldn't	[wʊdnt]
can not	can't	[kɑːnt]
must not	mustn't	[mʌsnt]
will not	won't	[wəʊnt]

1. Please, do**n't** take it the wrong way!
2. You do**n't** give your secretary enough credit.
3. It does**n't** work that way.
4. It wo**n't** matter anymore.

Lesson 44: Silent letters

C9
🎧 Words for silent "t"

Listen and repeat, noting that highlighted "t" is not pronounced.

whistle, wrestle, castle, thistle, often, soften, mortgage, gourmet, buffet, rapport

C10
🎧 Words for silent "h"

Listen and repeat, noting that highlighted "h" is not pronounced.

overwhelm, vehemently, whimsical, hour, exhibition, honourable, heir, honesty, vehicle, white, what

C11
🎧 Words for silent "w"

Listen and repeat, noting that highlighted "w" is not pronounced.

whom, answer, swordfish, wholesale, whose

C12
🎧 Words for silent "l"

Listen and repeat, noting that highlighted "l" is not pronounced.

calm, salmon, psalm, talk, half, could, should, would, walk, chalk, stalk, catwalk

C13
🎧 Words for silent "p" and "b"

Listen and repeat, noting that highlighted "p" and "b" are not pronounced.

p   psychology, receipt, psalm, pseudo-science, psychotic
b   bomb, tomb, thumb, dumb, doubt, doubtful, debt, doubtless

C14
🎧 Words for silent "o, i, a, e"

Listen and repeat, noting that highlighted vowels are not pronounced.

o	Cath**o**lic, choc**o**late
i	bus**i**ness, fam**i**ly
a	extr**a**ordinary, technic**a**lly
e	av**e**rage, ev**e**ry, ev**e**ning, pref**e**rence, temp**e**rature, int**e**resting, sev**e**ral, effectiv**e**ly

Lesson 45: Word endings

C14

🎧 **Voiced and unvoiced endings for plurals and third person singular [s] and [x]**

Rule: If the sound before the ending is unvoiced, then the ending will be unvoiced too. If the sound before the ending is voiced, then the ending will be voiced.

Plurals
[s]-[z]
rocks -rags
ranks-rings
cats-dogs
pets-pebbles
tapes-tables

Third person singular
[s]-[z]
works- warms
brakes- brings
sinks- sings
walks- worries
takes- tags

C15

🎧 **[ɪz] endings**

Rule: An extra syllable is formed by the short vowel [ɪ] (as in "pit") in plurals and words in the third person singular ending in "es". The result is that the "es" is pronounced as a voiced [ɪz].

Plurals
graces
kisses
losses
pieces
paces

Third person singular

reduc**es**
access**es**
los**es**
pass**es**
pleas**es**

C16
🎧 **Words for voiced ending [d]** "ed" at the end of a word can be pronounced as [t] or [d], depending on the sound preceding.

Rule: If the sound preceding the "ed" is any voiced sound, with the exception of [d], the "ed" is pronounced [d] (voiced).

live**d**, happene**d** , remembere**d**, pulle**d**, trie**d**, seeme**d**, handle**d**, haile**d**, remaine**d** , serve**d**

C17
🎧 **Words for unvoiced ending [t]**

Rule: If the sound preceding the "ed" is any unvoiced sound, with the exception of [t], the "ed" is pronounced [t] (unvoiced).

Listen and repeat the following words, noting the unvoiced /t/ ending:

helpe**d**, talke**d**, like**d**, aske**d**, watche**d**, stoppe**d**, walke**d**, passe**d**, wishe**d**, finishe**d**

C18
🎧 **Words for voiced ending [ɪd]**

Rule: If the "ed" is preceded by [t] or [d], an extra syllable is formed by a short vowel [ɪ] as in [pit]. The result is that the "ed" is pronounced as a voiced [ɪd].
Listen and repeat the following words, noting the voiced [ɪd] ending:

want**ed**, need**ed**, includ**ed**, creat**ed**, add**ed**, wait**ed**, expect**ed**, report**ed**, start**ed**, not**ed**

Lesson 46: Liaisons

The English tend to speak in phrases, rather than in separate words. They often link the words together. To sound fluent in English, liaise words that belong together in a phrase gliding from one word to another, almost pronouncing them as one word. Here are some basic rules to follow when liaising words together.

C19
🎧 Consonant elision

Rule: When a word finishes with the same consonant the next word starts with, we glide the two sounds into one with a slight pressure hold.

Listen and repeat the following word phrases, noting consonant elision.

no**t t**o mention, ro**ck c**oncert, fee**l l**onely, goo**d d**ay, las**t t**ime, drin**k c**ocktail, don'**t t**ell, kee**p p**rivate, re**d d**oor, ge**t t**ogether

C20
🎧 Liaison of vowel to vowel

Rule: When a word ends with a vowel, and the following word starts with a vowel, we link them together and pronounce them as one word.

Listen and repeat, linking vowel to vowel:

show off, throw in, do it, may I, my uncle, lie in, key in, pay in pounds, a few hours, so amazing

C21
🎧 Liaisons – Compound nouns

Rule: Link words in compound nouns, pronounce them as one word, stressing the first word in each phrase.

Listen and repeat, liaise words in phrases:

passport control, bus driver, travel bag, taxi stand, business deal, alarm clock, train station, foreign office, ticket machine, cash point

Lesson 47: Intonation and Sentence Stress

C22
🎧 Sentence rhythm: general rules
1. Do not separate words in a sentence; they should glide from one word to another like in a song. Avoid speaking in separate words. Speak in phrases where an article and preposition are linked to the main word.
2. When practising sentences stress the words which carry the most important meaning.
3. Often words with long vowels are stressed and sound prominent.
4. Do not stress articles or prepositions; pronounce them with a schwa [ə].
5. Often, unstressed vowels are pronounced with a schwa [ə].

Intonation/inflexion is a gentle rise and fall of the voice within a sentence. Learners of English are advised to listen to native English speakers on audio books, AUDIO TRACKSs, at the movies, in the theatre etc., and try to copy not only the pronunciation, but also the tune of the voice, or intonation.

Sentence Stress

The sentence stress depends on the meaning the speaker wants to convey:

Linda walked to the theatre with Michael.
Linda **walked** to the theatre with Michael.
Linda walked to the **theatre** with Michael.
Linda walked to the theatre with **Michael**.

Stress Analysis

1. By putting a stress on "Linda", we emphasise that it was Linda who walked to the theatre with Michael, and not somebody else.
2. By putting a stress on "walked" we emphasise that Linda walked to the theatre, and did not, for example, ride or cycle.
3. By putting a stress on "theatre", we emphasise that Linda walked to the theatre, and not to the cinema or a concert.

4. By putting a stress on "Michael", we emphasise that Linda walked to the theatre with Michael, and not with John or somebody else.

Lesson 48: Strong and weak forms of words

Certain words have two pronunciations. One we call the strong form, which is usually only used when the word is on its own or when it is stressed in a sentence. The other pronunciation, the weak form, is often used in a phrase or sentence if the word is unimportant and thrown away.

There is no consistent rule as to when you would use a strong or weak form. It depends on what message a speaker wishes to convey to his/her listener.

You will see from the sentences below, that we use the strong form when the word is important for the sense of the phrase. We use the weak form, on the other hand, when the word is unimportant and not stressed in a phrase.

C23
🎧 Sentences
The weak form of the words is pronounced with the schwa, which is highlighted:

1. **A**t the end **o**f the day, Linda w**a**s right about that.
2. T**o** tell the truth, I'm not very keen t**o** meet him.
3. It's **a**s true **a**s I'm standing here th**a**t my ex-husband has a girlfriend who is three years younger th**a**n me.
4. It's the height **o**f bad manners t**o** interrupt when someone is speaking.

C24
🎧 Comparisons

Stressed position/strong form, pronounced with a full vowel unstressed position/weak form, pronounced with the schwa[ə], which is highlighted:

I said I want eggs and bacon!
I'll have fish **a**nd chips.

What are you driving at?
I'm not driving **a**t anything.

As you already know...
It's **as** simple **as** that.

Did you really think that?
Yes, I thought th**at** it was alright.

What is he thinking of?
He is not thinking **of** anything.

Where has she come from?
She comes fr**o**m London.

I would... but I can't.
We can b**u**t hope.

What are you doing that for?
It's **for** you.

Have you seen her ?
I saw h**er** just now.

Is that you?
Who do y**ou** think you are?

Where are you going to?
I'm going t**o** work.

Is it us or them?
We could always ask th**e**m.

Passage: Product X

The weak form of the words is pronounced with the schwa, which is highlighted:

"Good morning, ladies **a**nd gentlemen, I've lots **o**f exciting things t**o** tell you about our new product. Because it's so new it'll h**a**ve t**o** be referred t**o a**s "Product X". Can you hear me **a**t the back? I can't speak too loudly in case there're industrial spies about.

I would love t**o** have brought a sample **o**f our new secret product t**o** show you but I couldn't because the inventor wouldn't release it, **a**s it's very secret. So you'll have t**o** take my word f**o**r it. I'll try **a**nd describe it t**o** you.

It's quite simply the most dramatic **a**nd innovative invention since the electric kettle.I hope I don't give too much away if I w**a**s to say I'm not sure how we could've managed if it hadn't been invented.

Many **o**f you will h**a**ve seen similar products on the market. That's not t**o** say they aren't quite good b**u**t I can state, without fear **o**f contradiction, that "Product X" is streets ahead **o**f our competitors.

Because **o**f the superior quality of "Product X" we sh**a**ll h**a**ve t**o** launch **a** highly sophisticated advertising campaign. F**o**r **a** start, we sh**a**ll probably need **a** celebrity, possibly someone fr**o**m "Big Brother", t**o** front **a** TV commercial. I c**a**n tell you no expense is going t**o** be spared in the world-wide exploitation **o**f our product; and, ladies **a**nd gentlemen, when we've achieved total market domination, you'll be able t**o** stand tall **a**nd say with pride, I w**a**s there when "Product X" w**a**s launched!"

Lesson 49: Natural flow of speech

In natural speech, it's important not to emphasize or stress too many words in a phrase or sentence. As a general rule, we tend to pick out the words which convey the meaning, and lean on them, giving them a little more vocal energy. The rest of the words, we "throw away" , an expression used by actors. This often means neutralising vowels, increasing the pace and diminishing the volume.

Task: Read the following sentences and dialogues out loud several times, giving the highlighted important words a little extra length and vocal power. Always make sure the "throw-away" words flow smoothly towards the stressed words. Stressed words are underlined.

C25
🎧 Sentences

1. You <u>know</u> because I've already <u>told</u> you that I <u>didn't want</u> to <u>go</u>.
2. The <u>cat</u> who was called "<u>Ginger</u>" was the <u>terror</u> of the <u>neighbourhood</u>.
3. If it hadn't been for the <u>rain</u>, the <u>wedding</u> would've been <u>perfect</u>.
4. From <u>my</u> point of view, the <u>whole affair</u> should've been <u>better managed</u>.
5. The <u>sport</u> was at its <u>height</u>, the <u>sliding</u> was at its <u>quickest</u>, the <u>laughter</u> was at its <u>loudest</u>, when a <u>sharp smart crack</u> was <u>heard</u>. (Pickwick Papers by Charles Dickens).

The Speech Organs

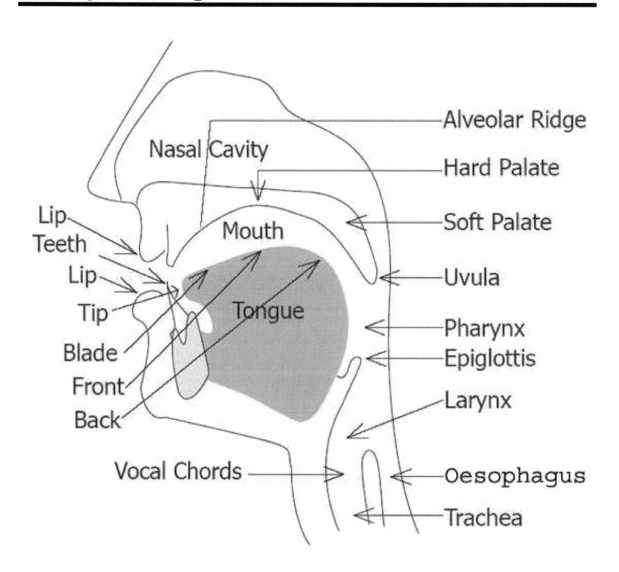

Tips and shortcuts to get rid of your accent fast!

1. Avoid speaking in your native language. Speaking in your native language will prevent you from memorising the correct placement of the speech organs and developing the speech organ muscles for the American sounds.

2. Avoid speaking too fast, pronounce every syllable. Many people are not able to make clear sounds when speaking rapidly and these lead to indistinct speech.

3. Read small sections from newspapers, magazines or books **out loud**. Audio books are fantastic to listen to and to imitate the correct pronunciation.

4. Do regular weekly recording exercises:
   - Record yourself reading,
   - Listen to your tape,
   - Make a note of sounds where you made a mistake in pronunciation,
   - Practice the sounds where you made a mistake with this book.

5. Learn poems and read them expressively; modulate your voice.

6. Join public speaking clubs such as Toastmasters, literature societies, and book clubs where you can speak out loud in public. See www.toastmasters.org for information.

Difficulties in pronunciation for speakers of world languages

As was outlined in the introduction, existence of an accent can be explained by the fact that some English sounds do not exist in your students' native language, and their speech organs are not trained for them. Therefore these sounds may represent a particular difficulty in pronunciation. Below we list speakers of world languages and their particular difficulties.

Main world language	Key countries where it is spoken	Particularly difficult English sounds	Recommendations
Arabic	Algeria, Egypt, Iraq, Jordan, Saudi Arabia, Syria, Tunisia, others	[r], [l], [tʃ], [ɔː], [ɜː], [ə]	Avoid aspirated trilled [r] **Lessons 41, 33, 42, 3, 5, 6**
Chinese	China, Taiwan, Malaysia, Singapore	[θ], [ð], [r], [au], [t], [d], [l], [n], [nd], [v] [eɪ]	Articulation exercises, particularly fricative consonants; give enough time to every syllable; connect sounds together, do not separate words into syllables. Pronounce final [t], [d],[l], [n], [v]; don't confuse [n] with [l] **Lessons 36, 37, 41, 23, 27, 30, 33, 30, 35, 17**

Main world language	Key countries where it is spoken	Particularly difficult English sounds	Recommendations
Czech and Slovak	Czech Republic, Slovakia	[w], [kw], [r], [θ], [ð], [æ], [I]	Do not lengthen vowels in second unstressed syllables. Avoid using [a:] for [æ] **Lessons 25, 41, 36, 37, 15, 33**
Farsi	Iran Afghanistan Pakistan	[θ], [ð], [w], [v], [æ], [l],[ʊ]	Avoid adding [e] before [s] **Lessons 36,37, 25, 35, 15, 33, 13**
French	France, Canada Caribien	[r], [i:], [ɪ], [j], [h], [θ], [ð], [ŋ] [l]	Avoid nasalisation of vowels when followed by [n] or [ŋ]. Anglicise words of French origin **Lessons 41, 4,7, 24, 40, 36, 37, 31,33**
German	Austria Germany Switzerland	[w], [r], [æ], [əʊ], [v], [d], [z], [θ], [ð], [l]	Be careful with voiced vs. unvoiced consonants **Lessons 25, 41, 15, 16, 35, 27, 38, 36, 37, 33**
Greek	Greece	[dʒ], [tʃ], [ʌ], [ə]	**Lessons 42, 9, 6**
Hungarian	Hungary	[r], [w], [θ], [ð], [əʊ]	**Lessons 41, 25, 36, 37, 16**
Hindu	India	[r], [w], [θ], [ð], [v], [eɪ]	**Lessons 41, 25, 36, 37, 35, 17**

Main world language	Key countries where it is spoken	Particularly difficult English sounds	Recommendations
Italian	Italy	[r], [θ], [ð], [t], [d], [ʌ], [ə]	Care needed on unstressed syllables and unpronounced letters **Lessons 41, 36, 37, 27, 9, 6**
Japanese	Japan	[l], [r], [θ], [ð], [ʒ], [t], [d], [əʊ], [ɜː], [s], [z], [ʌ], [ə], [dʒ]	Give enough time for each syllable **Lessons 33, 41, 36, 37, 39, 27, 16, 5, 38, 9, 6, 42**
Malay	Indonesia Malaysia	[əʊ], [ɔː], [ɜː], [æ], [θ], [ð], [ʃ], [ʒ]	Avoid over-pronouncing syllable clusters **Lessons 16, 3, 5, 15, 36, 37, 39**
Mongolian	Mongolia	[j], [l], [dʒ], [ʒ]	**Lessons 24, 33, 42, 39**
Nigerian	Nigeria	[r], [θ+ð], [ə], [ʌ], [ɜː], [ɔː], [v]	Avoid nasalization of vowels before final [n] + [m] **Lessons 41, 36, 37, 6, 9, 5, 3, 35**
Norwegian	Norway	[dʒ], [kw], [θ], [ð]	Work on voiced consonants **Lessons 42, 25, 36, 37**

Main world language	Key countries where it is spoken	Particularly difficult English sounds	Recommendations
Polish	Poland	[l], [r], [w], [θ], [ð]	**Lessons 33, 41, 25, 36, 37**
Portuguese	Portugal, Brazil	[l], [θ], [ð], [ʌ], [ə], [ʊ], [s], [z]	Pronounce [l] at the end of the word. Careful abou [s] and [z] at the beginning of the word **Lessons 33, 36, 37, 9, 6, 13, 38**
Russian	Russia, CIS countries	[l], [w], [ʃ], [t], [d], [n], [ŋ], [əʊ], [æ], [θ], [ð] [ɪ], [ɒ]	Avoid shortening long vowels, diphthongs, over-pronouncing consonants **Lessons 33, 25, 39, 33, 27, 31, 32, 16, 15, 36, 37, 7, 10**
Serbo-Croatian	Balkan countries	[r], [l], [æ], [e], [θ], [ð], [w]	Avoid de-voicing final voiced consonants **Lessons 41, 33, 15, 12, 36, 37, 25**
South Asian Languages	India Pakistan Bangladesh Nepal	[r], [w], [æ], [əʊ], [θ], [ð], [e]	Need to weaken the [r] sound **Lessons 41, 25, 15, 16, 36, 37, 12**
Swahili	Tanzania Kenya Uganda Zaire	Long and short vowels	**Lessons 1-15**

Spanish	Spain Latin America	[b],[v],[w],[h], [j],[dʒ] [r], [z], [ə], [ʌ]	Be sure to give full value to endings of words, and pronounce final consonants. Do not confuse[v] and [b], [j] and [dʒ], and [ʃ] and [tʃ]. **Lessons 26,35,25, 42,40, 24, 41, 38, 6, 9**
Swedish	Sweden	[w], [dʒ], [s], [z]	Work on voiced consonants **Lessons 25, 42, 38**
Turkish	Turkey	[θ], [ð], [r], [ə], [ʌ], [w]	Avoid over-pronouncing consonants **Lessons 36, 37, 41, 6, 9, 25**

Glossary

General

Articulation – The exercising and thus strengthening of the speech organs to produce sharp, crisp consonants, leading to good clear diction.

Intonation – The rise and fall of the voice in speaking.

International Phonetic Alphabet – An alphabet of symbols representing sounds.

Phonetics – The science concerned with the study of speech processes, including the production, reception and analysis of speech sounds.

Voice Modulation - Variation in the strength, tone or pitch of one's voice.

Sounds

Vowels – A vowel is a voiced sound which has a free passage of breath through the mouth and is shaped by different positions of the lips and tongue. There are twelve pure English vowels – five long and seven short.

Diphthongs – A diphthong is a voiced sound consisting of two vowel sounds glided together. There are eight diphthongs in English.

Triphthongs – A triphthong is a voiced sound consisting of three vowel sounds glided together. There are three triphthongs in English.

Semi-vowels – Speech organs start in the position of one vowel and immediately move to another vowel. e.g. [w], [j].

Consonants – A consonant is a sound formed by partially or completely stopping the breath stream anywhere between the larynx and the lips. There are several categories of consonants:

1. Plosives – The passage is completely blocked by speech organs, pressure is built up, and on sudden release an explosive sound or "plosion" is heard. e.g. [p]-[b], [t]-[d], [k]-[g].

2. Glottal Stop – A sound made when the vocal chords are closed tightly, not allowing air to flow through (like holding your breath or lifting something heavy).

3. Nasal – A sound formed by complete closure of the mouth, the soft palate being lowered, so that air is free to pass out through the nose. e.g. [m], [n], [ŋ].

4. Lateral - Air escapes round the sides of a blockage (tip of the tongue on the alveolar ridge). e.g. [l].

5. Fricatives - The air passage is narrowed so that the air in escaping produces audible friction or a kind of hissing sound. e.g. [f]-[v], [s]-[z], [h], [r], [θ] - [ð], [ʃ] - [ʒ].

6. Affricates – Have the first part Plosive followed immediately by the second part Fricative. e.g. [tʃ] - [dʒ].

Bibliography

Anthropology of British Tongue-Twisters by K. Parkin, Samuel French Ltd, 1969

The Complete Annotated Gilbert and Sullivan, Oxford University Press, 1996

Learner English by M. Swan and B. Smith, Cambridge University Press, 2001

Old Oxford Book of Verses and Tongue-twisters, Oxford University Press, 1969

Practical Phonetics by J.C.Wells and Greta Colson, Pitman, 1971

English Pronouncing Dictionary by Daniel Jones, Cambridge University Press, 1977

Clear Speech by Malcolm Morrison A. and C. Black. 1977

Modern English Pronunciation Practice by M.D. Munro Mackenzie, Longman, 1967

The Voice Book by Michael McCallion, Faber and Faber, 1988

English Phonetics and Phonology by Peter Roach, Cambridge University Press, 1983

The Right to Speak by Patsy Rodenburg, Methuen, 1992

A list of our accompanying apps

We have two iOS and two Android apps to help you master an English American accent and fluency. Below is the list of our elocution apps with their short descriptions.

We recommend that you start with the American Accent App and then move on to the Fluent American Speech app, because these two apps are essential for accent reduction.

Apps Functionality
All exercises are recorded on audio tracks that illustrate the model pronunciation. Students can play audio tracks, record themselves, and compare their pronunciation with the model.
The app is very easy to use. Simply touch the screen to play audio tracks, record yourself, and compare your pronunciation with the model.

1. **American Accent App**: this app is ideal if you want get rid of a foreign or regional accent and master Standard American accent. It has 42 lessons. It contains effective practical exercises to perfect all American English sounds.

2. **Fluent American Speech**: this app is a follow up to the American Accent App. It is ideal to develop fluency of your American English speech. It contains exercises for difficult and connected speech patterns, natural flow of speech, intonation and sentence stress.

These apps are for this book *Get Rid of your Accent Part One and Two, General American Accent Training Manual, ISBN 9780955330087,* the book is available on Audible.

Made in United States
Troutdale, OR
08/15/2023